STRAIGHT TALK
FROM THE
SHOWER GIRL

TABLE OF CONTENTS

Dedication 1

Introduction 4

Chapter 1 - In Your Beginning…... 18

Chapter 2 - Thinking Too Much?.. 22

Chapter 3 - Goal Setting…No, Realistic Goal Setting:....................... 24

Chapter 4 - When Your Why Changes.. 28

Chapter 5 - Excuses- You Will Be Looking For Them........................ 33

Chapter 6 - Keep Your Attitude In Check:... 42

Chapter 7 - Is Your Vision Blurred? 53

Chapter 8 - Branding Yourself 56

Chapter 9 - Recruiting For Longevity 66

Chapter 10 - Simple Why 76

Chapter 11 - Never Quit 77

Chapter 12 - Leading: No Title Needed 79

Chapter 13 - Learn From My Mistakes And Share Yours 83

Chapter 14 - Money- Are You Thinking 'Big Picture'? 88

Chapter 15 - Networking… The Only Constant.................................. 91

Chapter 16 - Preparing For Flight… 96

Chapter 17 - Customer Service And Sales Tips 98

Chapter 18- The Not So Secret Recipe………………………………….. 104

DEDICATION

When your fingers flow from your heart to the keyboard, there are no distractions or questions. This was by far the easiest part of the book to write. See, I haven't written it yet LOL.

I thank my parents for instilling in me my hard work ethic. That combined with the huge heart I was given, I am a huge force to reckon with. My childhood was far from perfect- I do not believe there is such a thing. Many say we are given what we can handle. I believe we are given what will help us grow. I grew up in an awesome place and my parents worked hard to get us there-that did not go unnoticed. I was taught to work for what I wanted when I was surrounded by people who were given quite a bit. I was taught when you try for something, nothing other than your best effort was acceptable. My mom always supported me while dad pushed- a perfect combo. So when you set goals, you really can't fail if you tried - truly tried. That is what I live by- not whether or not I reached the goal- but did I try my hardest? This, in turn, also showed me when you do try your hardest, you usually end up where you were aiming. And I was taught to love fiercely. And giving to others has always given me the most joy. Thank you, "Gramma and Grandpa"☺.

Talk about loving fiercely. My team. I got chills just typing those two words. Thank you, Team Why. I started this journey not even wanting to work with anyone. Every. Single. Person. On. Team Why Inc. Thank you. Not only did you trust me, learn from me, teach ME, laugh with me, challenge me, but you also gave me reason every single day to work harder than the last. There's no greater gift than being able to inspire someone to go after a goal. Whether that goal is a nice pair of shoes, a hidden bank account you were keeping to escape an awful spouse, or just wanting to be part of a group, I heard you. So much has been given to me in this journey, but it's the people I have met and the friendships I have made that truly have blessed me most -especially being surrounded by them during this shitshow 2020. To the over 174,000 people who have watched me sit in my shower and train, and yell a little, and smirk, wear weird accessories, spill my guts and shiver with excitement at the chance to help or inspire you, Shields in the Shower thanks you.

My boys…they hate me half the time. People say if your kids hate you, you are doing something right, so I must be a superstar. It's hard raising 3 boys. Three very different boys. Three amazing, loving, hard-working, adorable, funny, cuddly, too athletic, I could go on boys. I dedicate this to you. Everything I do is for you: My waking breath, wink, walk, thought is for you- pretty sure in my sleep, too. I know you've watched my journey and are proud. You tell me. Let me continue to show you how much I love you. I want to give you the world, that is why I work so hard. But, you have to learn how to earn it too. Love, hard work, and giving…we will start there. That's what I wish for you.

THEN AND NOW...STILL THE SAME "WHY" TO ME.

And to my company, where the little, normal people who needed a chance were given one. I needed a chance. I have been blessed by this company and my team because I have been giving them and it my all. It's come full circle and allowed me to be with my boys these past nine years and will continue to let me for however much longer my sons will acknowledge me. And as long as I am here, I will keep teaching in some kind of form. Where there is a will there is a way, and in my case, where there is a why, I will find a way. I have already sat in my shower, so where next?

*Thank **you** for supporting me and my boys by purchasing this book. I hope it helps you on your journey! Check out my website, a work in progress, where I have more info to share, lots of entertaining pictures I could not put in this book, a list of books that I recommend and learned from, and a whole lot of whatever I feel like having on my website. I would also love for you to leave me messages and feel free to ask me questions.*

Website: https://theshowergirl.com

Facebook: Heather McKay Shields

https://www.facebook.com/heather.m.shields.1/

Instagram: @heathershields

INTRODUCTION

Me: "Kids, this running around Nerf shooting is fine for now, but I have a work call in the shower in about an hour."

Rocco (10 years old): "Wait, Mrs. Shields, you work?"

Me: "Yes, honey."

Rocco: "But you're always here. You're always everywhere."

That was the moment I thought I had it all. I was a mom and a businesswoman. On my terms. And I love that the shower didn't even phase him.

I am a (now retired) Middle school English teacher who has earned over A MILLION dollars in a field that I had no training in, nor cared about to be quite honest, selling products that I knew nothing about, in a market that did not support me, having only ever sold Hallmark cards when I was in high school. How in the world is this possible? Oh, yes, all the while raising three INSANE boys of the ages 5, 3, and 1. I will, in a brutally honest way, be sharing all that I have learned with you during this crazy journey. I will not, however, be sitting in my shower, where I do all of my team training.

Plain old me …yup. I am not fancy, I am not special, I am not a genius, I am not money hungry…..All I WAS hungry for was the ability to take care of my boys. I was tired of being tired at school. Combine that with an opportunity, a great company, products that are in constant demand, a fun group of people, and a WILLINGNESS to learn, I made it happen. Anyone can with the right tools and attitude.

I like to say I am a self- proclaimed Jack Ass, and my most favorite thing to do ON THIS ENTIRE PLANET is to laugh. But, when it comes to doing all I can for my boys, I am a serious SOB. I guess this combo has lead to my success. But it's never just a combination of only two things. Nine years ago this month, I started with a direct selling company and it was the best decision of my life- I am so glad I was clueless as to what I was getting into. I may have been frightened away if I knew the true opportunity that was in front of me. Never be afraid to try something new. Never. Unless it's jumping out of a plane- don't do that- just my opinion.

> I got to the top.
> I had a Why…
> And here's the way…

Is this for you?

So recently, in a therapy session (yes, everybody who is alive in 2020 needs a therapist), Margaret said to me, "You have a story to tell. I am not sure how it's going to end, but I would read it!" This one statement, combined with hundreds of messages I have had in my inbox such as, "Your last training was like CPR for me," or, "You're a breath of fresh, true, air! I always look for you in the shower!" or, "You say it like it is and I really needed to hear it!"- has contributed to me typing today......I have finally typed the first paragraph. Are *you* ready to get moving?

And what better time to help people. Let's face it- the world has gone upside down in the last 6 months. No, not upside down- BAT shit crazy. Well, 'BAT' was a poor word choice. I don't need to list all the things wrong right now; I am sure you are feeling it in more than one area. What I DO know is that people are losing jobs, looking for kindness in the world, need another income, a positive distraction, and surely looking for things to relieve some stress.

If you want *something bigger* than you are experiencing now, this is for you.

If you have been told that *you couldn't do something*, this book is for you.

If you feel like *you are "stuck"*, this is for you.

If you want *to be pushed* out of your comfort zone, this is for you.

If you're craving to *be in control* of your own life, this is for you.

If you are not *sure who you are* as a brand, this is for you.

If you are in *direct sales*, this is for you.

If you *started a new job*, this is for you.

If *you HATE your current job*, this is for you.

If you think you are too "normal" to make some hardcore real money

If you are *seeking more friendships*, this is for you.

If you are *okay with some attitude* from an author, this is for you.

If you want to *become more confident*, this is for you.

If you have *gone after a goal* with no support, this is for you.

If you *want residual income*, this book is for you. If you do not know what "residual" is, Google it and then you WILL want to read this book.

If you are just curious about how a chick can sit in her shower and become *a million dollar plus earner*, read on to see all she's learned.

WHY this book?

I would be lying if I wasn't honest about a few other aspects that have come to head for me to finally sit down and start writing.

I am a hot-tempered, unfiltered speaker and words tend to fly out of my mouth. My friend Stephanie is the ONLY person I know who is more forward than myself, and she pointed out one day while on a walk how weird, yet awesome and inspiring it is to be able to sit in a shower and train people. That made me think because she is also very smart, down to earth, a hard worker, and someone I admire. Maybe I needed to listen to what she was saying. I always had notes and scripts for my shower trainings. So, I was already writing.

I love to teach, I love to help, I love to inspire……. I have been told over 100 times, "You need to write a book!" A book about what????……Do I write about my crazy life? How would that help someone? The craziness that comes with being a mom to three boys? Pretty sure if I wrote a book about MY three boys, it might have to be R rated and they may not like me in the end. Marriage? No expert there and marriage is hard enough -like I want to write about it. So, I am sticking to my passion - *teaching.*

I was a teacher for eleven glorious years in a wonderful middle school; seventh grade English, where I taught all ability levels. I cherished every second in front of the kids teaching them how to write and how to write with confidence. Man, I loved those kids. But once I had my third little boy and I was too tired to give those students my best, I quit. You'll hear more of the story as you learn through this book, but that is essentially where my journey to a million started.

SO now, I get to share with adults! I don't have to grade a gazillion papers. I don't have to deal with nasty parents who wonder why their kid got a C on their essay when really, they wrote it for them! I don't have to spend half my salary on daycare. In fact, I don't have to do anything I don't want to anymore UNLESS I WANT TO. BAM! Or should I say, DAMNNNNNN! What a feeling…and you can have that feeling, too. You have options. You do not have to work for others. Hence, me writing this for YOU. If these pages change one life like this business has changed mine, then these blisters from typing? Worth it. I want to share with anyone, regardless of the company you are in, that you can be VERY successful at anything with a lot of grit, a strong why, and not even a lot of grace- I am far from graceful.

There's another reason I am attacking the keyboard. Might as well be real honest while we are getting to know each other, correct? I find myself sucking down the wine lately - too much COVID craziness, being stuck at home, stress, maybe too much spouse time, and I love the taste LOL. Too much though is no good. Yes, we all know that many people love their wine, as I do, but I feel I need a new challenge to get myself on track. A new goal. Sooooooo, I made it to the top of my company and thought, "Now What?" A simple answer: This.

Why not help by sharing what I have learned and taught MY team with anyone willing to listen AND TRY?

Jess Carpenter
@JessCarpWrites

Can't wait to homeschool my kid while working from home while trying to eat healthy while avoiding the coronavirus while trying to keep sane while keeping up with the news while getting five minutes to myself while cleaning the house while writing a book while being a mom.

And It doesn't matter what you are, or are considering, "selling": what matters is your mindset, work ethic, and your reason (s). Are they big enough to get you where you want to be? We shall see. Mine weren't….at first.

Karma in a Bottle

To me, Karma is *real.* I live my life with "The More you Give the More you get" attitude. When I started to become successful in my industry and people asked, "Hey, Heather, would you mind popping on my team page and doing a little Q and A?" or "Hey, can I use you as a reward call if some of my teammates hit certain goals?" I NEVER said no, while many around me refused because it didn't directly benefit them time-wise or financially. Makes complete sense though. You really cannot blame them and that was their style. But for me, if I helped even a few I felt it would come back to me through the universe somehow. I am the kind of person who will take a stinkbug outside before I whack it dead. *Disclaimer -not fruit flies. Die, fruit flies, die.*

Here is an example of Karma that you can NOT disagree with...even though the return of karma was 20 years later. * *Disclaimer-Warning, you're going to get to know me a little here.*

I often reference the scar on my eyebrow. Mostly in videos or tutorials when showing products I am obsessed with. People have asked several times, "How did you get that scar? You never told us." I never told them because I either didn't know them well enough TO tell them or couldn't think of an exciting lie because the truth is embarrassing.

Freshman year in high school I was part of a group of friends. I liked most people, but I had a close niche. Well, a girl from another crowd was being nasty to us, to one of my friends, in particular, she seemed to focus on. We will call my friend Jaimie. We will call the nasty girl Mina. I got tired of Mina being mean and basically, a bully. One day after gym class, I saw Mina's hair spray bottle sitting on the bathroom sink. Hair spray was a daily part of our world back then- especially after gym class. It's like the 2020s dry shampoo obsession. I decided to give Mina a taste of nastiness back- I never let anyone mess with my friends. Have always been that way.

I peed in Mina's hairspray bottle.

Irrational thinking. But I had to go, she left it out, I had a why and she deserved a little payback. So, not sorry as it leads to greatness 20 years later.

Mina used it for three days before she figured out that there was giggling every time she squirted that tainted spray on her rolled back bangs. I was confronted and told her to leave my friend Jaimie alone or the contaminations had just started. Well, Mina punched me- purposely with a ton of rings on her fingers (wimp). Hence, a scar on the brow. Worth every stitch and she never bothered us, especially Jaimie, again.

Fast forward twenty years exactly. I joined this direct selling company. At first, I did not want to work with anyone or grow a team. One girl changed that all though! Guess who was the VERY first person to join me as a business partner? Yup- Jaimie. She signed herself up as my partner! Guess who is so successful she is a car earner which means big business? Yup. Jaimie. The world came full circle with a big fat thank you in the form of trust. And, it changed her life, too. And this partnership opened my eyes; *I learned that I could teach someone and make a difference.* This partnership changed the trajectory of my business

Just a funny "tinkle" of Karma in my life…every good act will be returned to bless you. The universe does not forget. Don't forget that. *Disclaimer- this does not mean go pee in peoples' things. Just showing you the gratitude that came back for being a good friend.*

So, putting down the glass, or better yet, box O'Shiraz, and writing to help even at least one of you who grabbed this book. Ignore my attitude, listen to what I have learned, and use it to grow. You can. I am no different than you.

Why "Shields in the Shower"?

A tremendous leader in my company had voluntarily started a Facebook page where brewing leaders were asked to hop on LIVE and train the entire company on a topic of their choice. Simple huh? Just a quick 20 minutes LIVE in front of strangers......

Barf.

Live?

Nerves.

I would have to stare at myself for 20 minutes.

No thank you.

But I was asked to. Back to that damn Karma thing. *If I just help one it will come back to me eventually*....OK, so I put my name in that infamous google doc with a date. No big deal, right? Sure- Just come up with training for maybe 130,000 people or so. I didn't feel like I was any different than anybody else, but I agreed to because I was asked to.

I said let's do it! Easy...except my children. Not just "children." That word sounds too proper. How do I hide from my boys who would certainly be running around naked, screaming at each other, or asking for my phone, nerf bullets flying around- and only nerf bullets if I was having a good boy mom day. Playing lacrosse in the basement, torturing each other, wedgies, or eating the entire box of Swiss Cake rolls while I was taking the time to train strangers.

I had one quick thought *hide in my shower.* Why my shower? My old bathroom was so ugly it was almost not real: Yellow tile, green toilet, scary built-in closets, beige stained carpet, and light fixtures fit for a haunted house ...the kids refused to go near it. The previous Easter I hid their Easter baskets in that prisoner like shower and the kids never found them after three hours LOL. We finally had to show them because they never looked; they were terrified of my bathroom... Even though we renovated it, they still tended to stay away.

I sat in my gorgeous new shower, plopped the phone on, hit that "live" button, and trained on something I felt powerful about- something that I could share that would teach another...it felt AWESOME. The positive comments and thank yous flowed in and I was done. I let it. all. out. the first. time. Heather Shields in the shower was born. ...clothed, of course. My new shower was my new space and my new love. Unexpectedly, the community of people who were in this Facebook training page loved what I had to say. And I quote Evan Darnell, "Heather Shields in the shower is my happy place."

Come Shower with Me!

What you will read in this book is the collection of any training I have ever done from my shower but strewn with details and examples that maybe you can relate to. I don't hold back because, well, no time for BS. Ever. If I can do it, you can. Over 174,000 people have watched me in my shower spill my knowledge and although this is not live and I am not in my shower, please know every word was typed with intent.

Intent to help. If it weren't for the books and the leaders that helped me grow, I wouldn't be here either. Creating this book with gratitude and Karma in mind. Someone who helped me might have someone who needs to read this book.

The TRUE meaning of Shields in the Shower:

But for all my shower viewers, it's much deeper than just a hiding spot. It has meaning. I just never shouted it out to the world because people wouldn't believe me, or I would seem materialistic or bragging- which is the furthest from me if you know me.

My new bathroom was gorgeous; the lighting, the marble, space, the white. The bathroom was completely paid for. I paid for that bathroom with one commission check. One. Something that would have been, after 11 years of teaching, one-fourth of my teaching salary. Every time I wanted to listen to my nerves and say no to doing another training, I remembered that commission check. If one of my shower videos helped even just one person earn extra money, it could make a difference. I could mean the difference between summer camp or no camp, a tutor or no tutor, a month's rent, or no rent....that is how you need to think. It could also mean helping someone's confidence, or focus, or if I can help steer just one away from the mistakes I made. It's not about the fancy bathroom...it is about what that extra income can mean to someone. Or the extra pride that is gained. To someone or someone's kid. To someone or someone's passion for giving. To someone or someone's parent. To someone you may never meet, but you can help. *That is the gift ...the gift of what any business can give if you work and you help others.*

I will never forget our Vegas convention, I believe it was the 5th one for me, when my husband came. He was never allowed before because, well duh, he was the babysitter while I went to our yearly convention. On the first day there, we had to walk a LOOOOOONG way from one end of the hotel to the other side. I counted 26....26 people stopped me and said, "Oh my gosh- are you Heather in the shower?" or "Can I have a picture- you are the shower girl!" My husband was like, "What the hell do you talk about in our shower?" I, very nicely said, "Well, maybe you should listen and learn!"

I learned a lot about myself that first time in the shower. I learned I have something to say. I learned I had something to teach. I learned that with a click of a live button I could impact thousands. I also learned what got me moving was still that "Thank you" from teaching. It just, for this chapter of my life, was thank you praises from people like me who needed a change, not from 7th-grade students. It was time to help others who wanted MORE...just as I did. More what? Well, that's what YOU need to figure out.

How in the world did I get into "this" direct selling?

I was hired and teaching straight out of college at the age of 22. I taught Language Arts for 11 years to 7th and 8th graders in an awesome school in Maryland. I loved every second of it…..until I had kids of my own. I got tired. I was burnt from the endless frontal teaching and grading essays. I was annoyed with some of the parenting BS I had to deal with. I was tired of not being paid what I was worth. I always said teachers need salaries for teaching the kids and a separate salary for dealing with their parents. I was tired of seeing others slack. I was tired of being tired at home.

So I went on "child-rearing leave" with the intent of probably not returning but the option was there for the next nine years. Handing in that leave letter was terrifying. Teachers are awesome and the ones I had worked with for eleven years WERE MY FAMILY. And, to leave a secure tenure teaching job with great benefits and summers off? Yup. I didn't have a choice. I told my husband when we got married that if I can't be the best teacher then I would give my position to someone who could be. And I wanted to be a better mom, so the answer was there already. Little did I know a new family was awaiting me where I could also teach, make a lot more money, and be my own boss. And the best part? I had no idea about this when I started.

So, ask yourself, are you tired? Are you tired of where you currently are? ***The riskiest place to be is in the same place.***

Fast forward eight weeks from the day I turned that resignation/leave letter in, we packed up and moved to Pittsburgh, Pennsylvania where many of our close friends and family had been living. Where both my husband and I grew up. Where the cost of living was a lot less expensive. Where education was awesome. Where I could be that stay at home mom that I so wanted to be.

Or so I thought. Not even two months into being that stay at home mom that I dreamed of being, I was going crazy. I was used to working and working hard...so thinking about chicken nuggets and the laundry all day was just not cutting it for me. I was confused. My mind needed something for me. That's when I was introduced to direct selling and my company; one magical little sample in the mail.

> On Being a Stay at Home Mom:
>
> Half of the time I feel like I'm running an insane asylum...the other half I feel I belong in one.
>
> your ecards
> someecards.com

Jenn, a girl from high school I knew of but was not close with (she was older- I always have to say that LOL) had been following me on Facebook...such a smartie. Jenn had just lost her pharma job and found this company by watching one morning when it appeared on The Today show, as it just so happened to be featured that day. She immediately joined and got to work. Jenn had been following me because she knew I had left teaching, she knew I had moved to a new area, and she was immediately following the recipe for success which you will learn here- it is a recipe. No magic ingredients. No luck. No 'right timing'. Drives me nuts when people say, "Oh you just got in at the right time." People say that to make themselves feel better cause THEY couldn't hack it. Sorry, not sorry.

I reacted to a before and after picture she posted on Facebook and sent her a message. My skin was horrid, and I was looking for help. Jenn sent me a little sample in the mail of some kind of paste for the face and it exploded in the envelope. But I used it! I used it and loved it. I loved it so much that I went into that bathroom trash can the next day to scrape any leftovers out of that envelope! Yes, it was that good.

I told her I loved it. Next thing I knew, this girl was calling me. I initially intended to not even answer, but I did. Twenty - five minutes later, credit card in hand, I bought a kit. Like, a kit to start the business, not even just a box of the product I wanted to try. I bought the whole damn thing $695.00 later so I could save the most on all of the products. Totally normal for me- I am a cheap ass. I had no intention of becoming a true active consultant, let alone becoming very successful, but several things happened over the next year. The first that happened was seeing the product work- like legit fixed my face. The best investment of my life and I didn't even know it when I shoved that pricey brown FedEx box into my closet.

Here we Grow!

What have I talked about in the shower that so many enjoyed or learned or needed to hear? Here we go…in NO particular order. I did not want to spend the time figuring out what I thought was an appropriate outline since all of our journeys are different. I wanted to write and get this book out there because *people are needing and looking for opportunities*. And at my level in my company, I know what is next for me and I am geeked! Every person who picks up this book is most likely in a different chapter of their own anyhow, but the one thing you ALL HAVE is the opportunity TODAY to DECIDE to get to work…if you want it. Half the battle is deciding, the other half is all in this book. Of course, this is my unique story. Not as shocking as nothing about me is normal☺.

CHAPTER 1 - IN YOUR BEGINNING....

I remember the first time I told my husband, "Hey- I think I am going to sell this stuff!" And he replied as he stood in the hallway in his tighty whities, "What? Heather, you can't sell sh—." Granted, he's a great salesman and he didn't even know I was using the product and loving it, so I did see where he is coming from. Teacher certified, crazy busy with kids, and never part of a business and you want to hop out into the world and sell skincare? I am glad I did not take his comment to heart, but I am sure glad he said it.

My first lesson was learned. **MAKE an "I told you so List"**.

The husband was the first on my list! Physically sit down and write on paper the name of anyone who laughs at you. Anyone who you want to prove wrong. Any person who says you can't do it. Make sure you include the names of people that need to see your success. Any person who does not support you. Make it. Make that list with vengeance. **They are out there**; know this now, and some of the names may surprise you. It feels good to write them down and visit the list often for an extra push when you stall.

My husband's belief that I couldn't do this business lit a fire under my ass…like a legit blow torch. I was just going to share and make some side cash. He should be supportive of anything I do. Right? *Disclaimer- in the perfect Fakebook world.* I was grateful for that statement from him though- it got me simply moving. How many people buy into something and then never step foot into the new business? Plenty. Sadly, more than plenty. "Let me show you, dear hubby," set in and I was off to the selling field. Make your list and start **proving them wrong**. It' so gosh darn fun to be right.

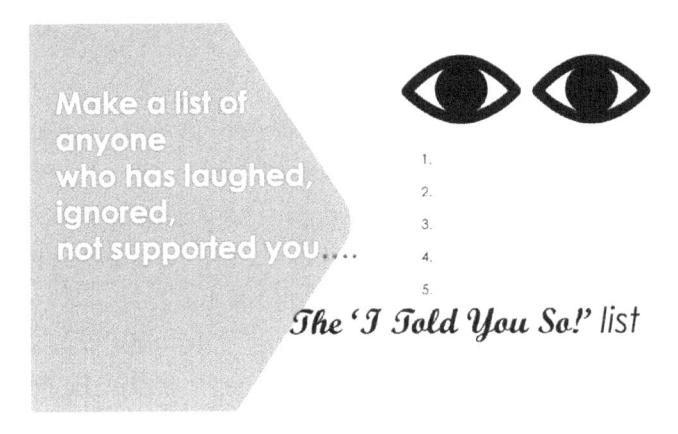

Make a list of anyone who has laughed, ignored, not supported you....

1.
2.
3.
4.
5.

The 'I Told You So!' list

I made my mind up to get working. Cool! I was excited to start. But- the big B.U.T. word- *I didn't know everything.* That crossed my mind for about two seconds. All of this was just for some fun. What did I have to lose! Who starts a job and knows everything day one? Nobody that I know of, but they still get that paycheck once or twice a month.

With any job or any company, you can **"Earn as you learn."** Jenn started me off in the best way possible- she told me what to do. Jenn never asked she simply guided me, "This is what you're doing." First, I had to host what we THEN called a launch party. We know "party" is a dirty word- nobody wants to go to a party expecting to whip out a credit card and be forced to order something. That's an entirely different chapter.

She drove eight hours to help me with this "launch party". I handmade invitations, I invited everyone local I knew, and I looked at the information about all of our products MAYBE twice if we want to be honest. I knew she was running the show, so I didn't overly prepare- plus I only wanted to do this to distract the chicken nuggets right? Well, she did make me get up and talk for a little in front of some friends and my family. I started talking about our one line that helps with sensitive skin. I explained how my dad loves this awesome 4 step system, I knew it was a green box, and I knew that it helped my dad's skin get relief. Yup. Smooth, I was describing. Nope. Wrong name. I stood in front of my friends and family and made a fool of myself, or so I thought. People still purchased it. Why? Because they wanted what the product promised to do.

I learned a lot that night. I learned some people WILL **support you.** I had invited maybe 75 people and about 17 total showed, but it was enough to force me to get moving and proved that people wanted the products that I now had to share with them. I also learned that that one launch evening was *not the predictor* of my future business. It was simply a starting date. An **official opening date-** just as salons and restaurants have when those big red ribbons are cut. In the beginning, **launch your business. Share it** with your friends and family in person and virtually. Believe that people want your stuff- why wouldn't they? I wanted it! And do not think you have to know it all, or you will never truly get going.

Nine years in and at the top of my company, I still don't know everything that is in our products; I know they work, and I know we have the ingredient lists available to all clients with a touch of a button. Rather than memorize and fret, I spent my time **moving through more** people and letting them know what premium skincare I had to share. *Say less and move more* should be on your mind. There are a lot of people on this planet you could move through.

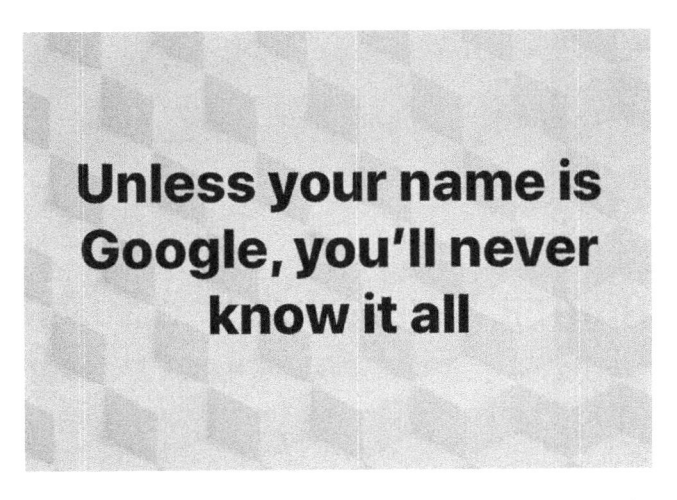

> **Unless your name is Google, you'll never know it all**

The regimen that I first tried completely changed my face- all from my bathroom, no doctors' visits, no copays, no pain. All from home. Who wouldn't want that? That's what I SIMPLY remembered in the beginning. You can make your journey as simple or as complicated as you want. **Be simple!** You are the one in control.

If you're waiting to learn more, you're making an excuse.

CHAPTER 2 - THINKING TOO MUCH?

My teaching itch started in college, sort of by accident I guess you can say. When I started looking at colleges, I was certain I would get into Penn State. I went to a great high school, had good grades, and lived in the state. Easy entry and I thought I had the acceptance in the bag, right?

Wow- that rejection letter came back so fast that I am not even sure it was opened. "Sooooo where now?" was thrown in my face. I remember sitting in the guidance counselor's office and in one hour had a college in mind. I chose Towson University in Maryland because of the not too far distance, it was a good nursing school, and was within my budget. I wanted to be a nurse, or so I thought until I had my blood taken at a physical and got sick at the sight of red. I decided I might as well change my major to teaching since Towson was also a good teaching school and I couldn't stand the sight of blood which would most likely be an ongoing issue as a nurse. That's how simple I thought from choosing a school to switching professions in the matter of two experiences- which, in turn, is a huge component of my success as you will see.

I **never pressured myself when I started** this side business. I truly just wanted Target money and something to think of while home all day *loooooooooong*. That's it. My full-time job was being the stay at home mom I wanted to be and that is why I left a teaching job I loved. Some extra spending money for me while the boys chugged Slurpees at Target was a bonus. No big deal. I TRULY believe this nonchalant attitude played a HUGE role in my success. Everything I earned was extra! My first commission check $357 bucks! Awesome! For what? Drinking boxes of wine with some friends and family, mispronouncing some products and adult time? I was hooked. Ask yourself, **"What kind of pressure are you putting on yourself?"** Especially in the beginning.

My second commission check was $0.00

I was so embarrassed because I knew how easy it was to get at least that $300 and then right to ZERO? Ouch. Ego loss. I learned quickly that you had to *do* stuff. I did nothing during my second month in business. That right there was when I vowed to never have a zero commission check again and to strive for a larger one each month- even if it was only ten dollars more- *try for more*. And that simple self-challenge I did month after month is when I started to see my business slowly grow.

I wanted larger commission checks. Maybe it was just because of the competitive nature in myself, or maybe because I knew what little you had to do for commission earnings versus $0. For me, I needed some tangible THINGS to work for. Maybe for you, your extra is a purse, or fancy shoes, or a person to help clean, or babysitter for nights out, pay for the family's food bill, or summer camp (which is a vacation for you)!

What do you want???? It's perfectly normal to want things. *What's not okay is putting pressure on yourself if your current goals and your work output do not align.* You can't WANT a four-digit payout, put out little to no work, and be mad at yourself because you failed. That equation will crush you before you even realize where you went wrong. **Realistic starts with small.**

CHAPTER 3 - GOAL SETTING...NO, REALISTIC GOAL SETTING:

Goal setting_includes deciding what you want – in life, in your business, in your wallet, in your heart, or any combination. One key element to having a goal(s) is to identify them, write them down, and share them with others. Write down WHAT YOU WANT. That is the first step with goal setting. But your goals, learn now, need to be **S.M.A.R.T** or you will self- deplete if you do not achieve them.

What do you want? LIST ten things you want below.

Look at your list above. If your first goal is to retire yourself or your spouse, move it to the last spot right now. If your first goal is to earn a $25 commission check erase it and up your game.

Now, list them in order from the smallest goal to the largest goal. What is the easiest to achieves versus what will be most challenging?

Wanting to retire yourself or spouse is an awesome, and an achievable goal, but not as your first one! It's okay to focus on your long-term goal/vision, but you need to set and accomplish smaller goals that will move you towards the ultimate want. Think of it as a ladder. Do you want that free car from the company or that vacation? Awesome, but it won't happen in month one. If someone is proclaiming you can, wave goodbye and find a person who tells you it will be hard, but it will be worth it. What smaller, more attainable goals can you *reach along the way* that will be stepping-stones to that car or trip or retirement? **Realistic goal setting sets up for success** rather than discouragement.

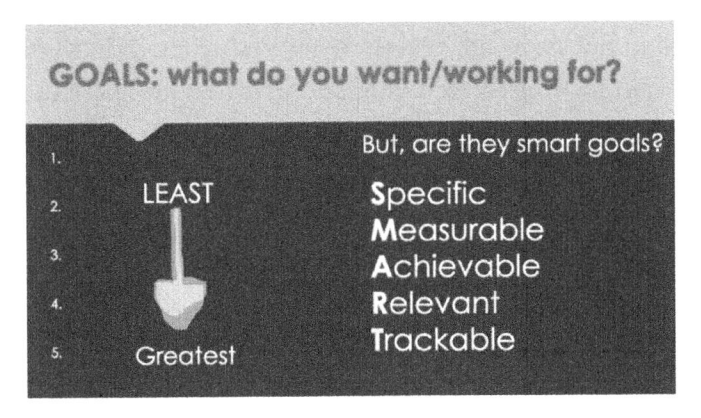

GOALS: what do you want/working for?	
	But, are they smart goals?
1.	**S**pecific
2. LEAST	**M**easurable
3. ⬇	**A**chievable
4.	**R**elevant
5. Greatest	**T**rackable

Be incredibly specific when setting goals, but also make sure your goals are targets **THAT YOU CAN CONTROL**. Often, goals are written down and worked for when in reality the person has no control over them! Here is an example of a goal that you CAN'T control, setting you up for failure.

"My new business partner will promote three times and gain 11 customers."

Take that unrealistic goal and write it so it's IN your control. This is unrealistic because you can't MAKE someone promote or MAKE them get anything.

Revamped goal: *"I am going to help my new business partner host two events, aim for eight new customers, and find new business prospects. I am also going to guide her with her social media, and I will host a virtual product demo for her friends and family."*

You might be thinking 'Wow that second one is a lot!' But do you see the difference? You can't fail at the goal of helping your new partner and setting up some activities to promote with an attempt to gain clients. But if you say, "THEY WILL promote" *with no plan*, you will blame yourself when they do not achieve. The downward spiral would begin.

On the other hand, if you executed the plan that was put in place, helped with ALL of those activities you listed above, your goal was met. You may not have hit exactly what you wanted, but your business grew, your partner appreciated you, and you're both ready to tackle next month.

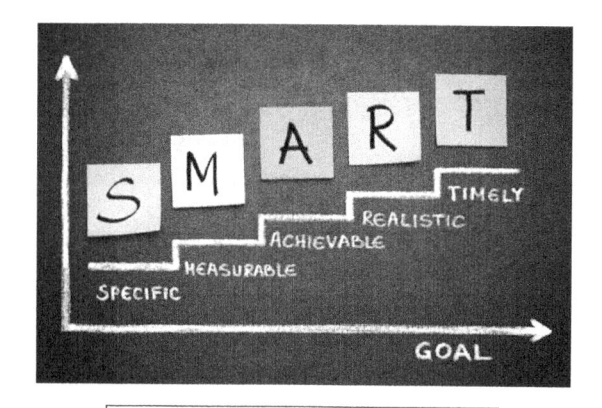

*Disclaimer- pick your "T". I prefer 'timely'...be realistic with how long a goal could take.

Goals are a way to *break down your vision* into *manageable* and *achievable* steps. For example, if you want to take your loved ones to Disney World, you need to determine how much that trip will cost. Once you know the dollar amount, you can plan what you are going to need in commissions per month, then 4 months, then 8, etc .? Are you shooting for next year? If so, what will you do each month, 12 months, to get that monthly commission? What will be your PLAN? It is frustrating when people think they can simply post on social media and pray and money will show up. Work a plan. Plan it out. Execute with your best efforts. DO everything in your plan and you succeeded. Make a crazy goal and do nothing, you'll fail.

You have to also ask yourself are these goals attainable? But more importantly, are you willing to do the work it may take to achieve them? Very often what someone wants doesn't align with what he or she is willing to do. Stretching is important for personal growth and income growth; however, being realistic and asking yourself if you are up for the challenge is critical, as well.

Take a look below....This is my actual goal list from years ago.

1. Target money
2. Dresser
3. Pay for Christmas
4. Mortgage so we could move
5. Family vacation
6. Free Napa trip from company
7. The car
8. Master bathroom
9. New kitchen
10. No debt

These were the things I WANTED. Once I achieved one, I upped the next goal (whether it was an actual thing, experience, or monetary).

CHAPTER 4 - WHEN YOUR WHY CHANGES

Man, I love that list. Sorry- a little self- reflection there for a minute. Target money. I just wanted that money to blow on whatever I did not need. The typical Target spree. The $350 a month and more challenge for myself was great until I saw this gorgeous dresser. I had to have it. It was expensive. I don't do expensive. Perfect- this money I am making from this little side gig IS ALL EXTRA so I can justify that dresser. I can buy it with this fun money I am earning- guilt-free. A few months later, I got that dresser $900 sold! I kind of felt like I was getting it for free remember? I was home. My full-time job was the boys…feeding them, entertaining, hell, keeping them alive let alone stitch-free. I did it! Cashed that pay and went right to the furniture store. My entire bedroom is decorated around that dresser and I wake up every morning staring at it. An awesome daily reminder of how small I started.

My next mission was Christmas. I wanted to be able to pay for all of the holidays. That was a very emotional goal to set let alone hit. I can completely still visualize the tree surrounded by beautiful gifts. They were annoying boy toys, all things boys, but they were so pretty to me because I paid for EVERY single thing under it.

First family vacation on me! Hello, airplane rides and Florida sand!

Here is where it all changed and it wasn't pretty. Seven months after we moved to Pittsburgh for my husband's job, right after I gave up an awesome stable teaching job, right when I moved that dresser into my house, he was fired. Out of the blew, unexpected, and he was doing very well. Blindsided. No other words. He was in a tough industry and this just made our life a whole lot tougher.

In a matter of 48 hours, my why for joining the networking industry drastically changed. The desire for monthly spending money and something to think about turned into what had to be "it" for me. I will never forget when he told me about losing his job. We were sitting in an office with our son and a counselor at an appointment. He told me about his being fired in front of a stranger …My husband was smart. He knew I would be devastated. He also knew that I couldn't kill him in front of a counselor. The counselor said, "Oh I am sorry- are you telling her here for the first time?"

Silence the entire way home. Silence in my car- thank god we had two cars and drove separately. I was in such shock I couldn't even cry until I was home.

I cried for twenty-four hours straight. Then Panicked. It was the worst day of my life. I felt helpless. I felt I failed my kids- how was I going to take care of these three gorgeous humans I brought into this world? I just left the perfect teaching job to be home with them. I am responsible for them. I was devastated.

That was the day. That was the day I decided that skincare was going to be "it" for me. For me and my family. The answer for me. I made the decision. I couldn't go back to teaching in Maryland. I wouldn't get hired in Pennsylvania....I was too experienced, which means expensive, and there were no positions. I knew that teaching for me was over. And. I. Was. Not. Leaving. My boys.

Girls that joined this company before me were killing it in NYC. They were leaving jobs, earning cars, earning trips, so why not me??? It didn't take a brain surgeon to realize if they are getting free cars an trips, they must be earning quite a bit. There was my new vision- kicked fun money right out the door and welcomed, "stability". I felt my low, and I never wanted to feel it again. I knew I could make money- I already had. I knew it was fun- I was loving it. I knew the products worked- they fixed my face. And I knew people wanted them. Time to *REALLY* get to work.

It was a Decision…and it is for you, too.

As hard as that 24 hours of sobbing till my eyes swelled was, maybe it was a blessing. It kicked my ass into real gear. My blow torch flame just became a raging comet's tail. If he had never lost that job, maybe I would still be shooting for Slurpee money or Christmas, and not the stability this company has given me.

Are you paycheck to paycheck and sick of it? *Then decide.*

DO you think your job, or significant other's job, is %100 secure? *Wrong decision.*

Are you busting your butt in a job that doesn't recognize or appreciate you? *Then decide.*

Tired of the daily rat race and working for another? *Then decide to change.*

It's a decision. But it's only a decision that matters if it is followed with the motivation. Motivation to try something else. Motivation to make something else work. Motivation to run the marathon for a true change, not the sprint for a temporary cushion.

And the truth can be harsh sometimes. I like harsh. I call them "love smacks". You don't need more time in your day, you need to decide. Those girls killing it in NYC had the same hours in a day I did. They had the same resources, the same websites, the same pieces of training, selling the same products, maybe they just had more of a why. **So be a goal-getter…**

First, they decide.

Then, they make smart goals.

Then they make plans or a roadmap.

Then they do the work.

…they do the work daily.

They reflect.

They continue to do what is working and they stop doing what is not working.

They lead.

They take *every* opportunity to grow.

They do things they don't want to do.

They get uncomfortable.

They GO and they grow.

My favorite shirt

CHAPTER 5 - EXCUSES- YOU WILL BE LOOKING FOR THEM

Now that you have decided to go for it, or do this, or whatever you're going after, you will start to look for excuses as to why you can't. Or why it won't work. Or what will stop you from succeeding.

If you are restarting or revamping your business, it's important to identify the excuses you will use or have used...You know yourself. The past is a predictor of the future IF you continue to do the things you've always done. **You need to get honest with yourself** about what got in the way. It's easy to blame the family, the economy, or the weather, but the truth will most likely be something more personal to you, such as a fear of or resistance to doing what needs to be done. Don't skip this step, so let's look at some common excuses and defunct them now. *Disclaimer- I had someone tell me they couldn't go to an event because it was raining.*

It took me two hours to sit down and start writing this morning. The kids are actually IN SCHOOL for two days this week (go away COVID), I should be chomping at the bit to get to this computer. I just made myself an omelet. I haven't made an omelet for myself in...actually, I never have. I did a load of towels. I hate laundry. I made a grocery list, which is a complete waste of time because my delivery service knows what I buy. *I am looking for excuses* to not sit down and. get. this. Done. Why? Because I am terrified.

I am terrified that maybe not one person will buy this book. I am terrified that someone may read it and give it a bad review. I am terrified of failure. SO instead of sitting down and facing the fear that this may account for nothing, I pretend to be the mom of the year by doing homely things. You have to do hard things. Acknowledge them, attack them, and get moving.

So #1 the fear of failure is real. I get it. But I also got over it. You know why? If I found myself failing, it was usually because I was DOING a lot. If you're making mistakes you are moving, and you have to move with any business. I suggest you fail as much as you can and that means **you are failing forward.** If you are succeeding at EVERYthing you are doing, you most likely are not pushing yourself out of your comfort zone. You don't go, you don't grow.

The other great part about making mistakes is you can share them with others. What did not work for you might work for someone else, so when you are open about making mistakes, you're also supporting each other without even knowing it. I am perfectly imperfect and am constantly striving to make mistakes. Fear of failure is simply an excuse to NOT DO the hard things.

If you're feeling nervous about something, you should do it. That means you are uncomfortable. If you are putting off something because you are not fully prepared, you should do it. You will never be 100% prepared.

Grow a set Activity:

Write five things below that make you scared! I want to see you do something you're afraid of! (Go to my website listed at the end and tell me, so I can celebrate your bravery and coachability. I have always had balls… maybe that's why I got all boys). Just go do them!

Afraid of a live video

Asking your BFF???????

_____

_____

_____

_____

_____

_____

_____

#2 excuse. *One hard aspect of everyone's life is a lack of support.* If you're afraid of taking on something because **"Nobody will support me!"** **BLAHHHH**! Here are two what I refer to as ' love smacks'.

First of all, *ARE THEY PAYING YOUR BILLS?* The people that you are worried about, or worried about what they think, do they legit provide for you and your family? No. And the truth is, those people you are fearing who may pass judgment don't think about you for more than a nanosecond. You are wasting more energy on worrying about them than they will ever care about what you are doing. Stop caring about the non- supporters. They aren't thinking about you. Put them on your 'I Told You So' list and move on.

Secondly, those people who don't support you are probably not nice. I mean, someone who genuinely cares about you will support you in whatever you do. **So, find astonishing or positive people and hang out with them.** You choose who you spend time with. Again, a choice, so *get rid of the assholes.* Non-supporters are usually jealous, ignorant, or just don't care enough to acknowledge what you are doing. Have a date soon with someone who is negative or doesn't help? A more productive use of your time would be to cancel those plans and watch an episode of "Shark Tank" or "Undercover Boss". Seriously. Those shows will motivate you. Even "Naked and Afraid"! Whatever you are afraid of is not harder than living in the woods naked, with a stranger, eating bugs.

Reassess your relationships and minimize dramatic people in your life. If hanging out with someone leaves you exhausted, like you just watched an entire season of Real Housewives of Atlanta, take that as a sign to stop interacting with them as much. Low-accountable people may appear to work hard, yet find complaints about everything. They come to believe that making them happy is someone else's job. **BYE, Felicia.** There are many out there.

My favorite people!

#3. You aren't confident. I have not met one person who starts any journey confidently. Confidence comes from **LEARNING, ATTEMPTING, AND SUCCEEDING.** You know that saying, "Grow some balls"? Well, your balls come from guts and glory. *The bravery to*

try and then the warm and fuzzy feeling when you win. So this is excuse is a lame one. To gain confidence, there are two things you can do right away. Like close this book and go find some leaders in your industry to follow. Do what they do. Simple. Let them lead you. And second, read books- oh wait you are- well done☺. Guess nothing more to say there. I have a list of books on my website with suggestions and I have read a bazillion.

#4. If you're lacking confidence, perhaps **you are lacking some self-esteem**. I have to tell you honestly, I had very low self-esteem when I signed on. I was overweight. I was crazy trying to sell when I had an education degree. But I knew I could talk, and I knew that I could not let the lack of self-esteem stop me from doing what I needed to do. Providing for your kids is a pretty big task to carry on your shoulders, so the extreme me decided to make a change. *Disclaimer-I love this story you are about to read. I needed to attack the weight. It hindered every part of me.*

So, I went to a fat doctor ...by accident. Okay, that may be confusing... When I DECIDED that I was running hard with this business, I hit the streets. I would get clothes on, real clothes not yoga pants, like dressed up. I would walk into salons and pitch to the owners. I would make spa appointments just to get into places and introduce them to my products. I would get my hair cut anywhere that had an opening and just to sit in a chair for an hour and talk about my products. Well, walking down a strip mall one day I saw a sign for "Lose weight here". You bet your butt I walked in. I walked in intending to just meet people, hand them my cards, and making connections. A fancy way of saying I was networking. I knew a doctor had to be in there somewhere.

The next thing I know, I am sitting in a chair having my blood drawn and filling out paperwork. I sat in a chair so I could have a long conversation with a nurse. "This was an opportunity" my mind was screaming. I loved her! I wanted more time with her. Erica was her name. Sure- stick a needle in my arm, take my blood, let's chat it up! See- I was obsessed with the potential early on. This fat loss place had a program called HCG. It was an extreme program where you take shots and eat 500 calories a day and you lose a pound a day. Oh, and it cost a fortune. But I LOVED Erica.

I was able to get my blood drawn that morning since I had not eaten. I ended up going back after my blood result returned healthy enough to try the HCG program. But I also wanted Erica on my team or at least a customer. She was a nurse (score), witty (good personality), had a kid (works hard), I thought she'd be perfect.

Long story short, I ended up losing 40 pounds. Forty freaking pounds. The doctor in the office ended up joining my team. Mission accomplished. Nothing came of him, that's another chapter you will hear later, but years later I found Erica on Facebook. She is on my team, and we are friends, so I got my Erica. I put back on the 40 pounds but am working on making real weight loss choices now and I am currently down 20. 20 over three healthy months not shots and eating lettuce and air. So, I went off there on a tangent, sorry. The point was, I lost the weight and man I got confident. I wanted to get out more, talk to people more, the way I spoke, and carried myself changed.

If something is holding you back self-esteem wise, identify it, and tackle it. You will learn a lot about yourself on the way. In turn, you'll grow in business, too. And get yourself a Margaret! Admit when you are using an excuse. Face your fears and force yourself to be uncomfortable. If your Why is large enough, you will. And working on yourself with personal development is never a bad thing whether it is for business or not.

Disclaimer- the following is just a little inspirational break to keep you reading as I get a little bit harsher.

My life Before my Business Success: (11 years of teaching)

Sneak out before their sweet faces wake at 6 am. They, my beautiful boys. Tears would stream down their cheeks if they saw me leave in the morning. So instead of them seeing me, I would get up at 5:30 am and leave before my loves could even catch a glimpse. How freaking sad to type this, let alone live it every single day.

Not sure if they even ate breakfast.

Drive an hour to my school, praying I wouldn't fall asleep at the wheel.

Teach all day…teach a lot and teach a lot of kids.

Fall asleep driving home.

Go right to the gym and walk out after ten minutes. I couldn't be there away from my kids another minute longer.

Pick up my boys and make dinner and play maybe an hour…but the whole time I was worried about the papers to grade and plans for tomorrow and waking again only to leave them.

Kiss them for bed- nearly three hours after I picked them up because they were so tired from their school and daycare.

I grade papers all night and the cycle starts over.

After success with my business: I am in year 9, Glorious 9….

I wake with my kids…every morning.

Drink my hot coffee…reheat however many times I need to cause it's my schedule.

Make them breakfast. One a strudel, one Nutella waffles, and one egg wrap.

Get them on the bus

Work for an hour, 2 maybe all day.

Run any errands.

Volunteer at the schools or host field trips if they wanted me there.

Be home for them off the bus (would sneak in the gym or spin three times a week, not daily, that would be a lie).

All sports activities…always a mom who drives wherever. I love it. During long-ass baseball games, yes I would work on my phone.

Make dinner and do homework and I work while they do. I just liked sitting with them.

Phone calls and zooms at 9.

What's your day look like? What would you want it to look like? What would you change?

You don't have to write it here, but I am asking you to chat with yourself about this. My husband talks to himself. Fact, it's a little weird. I asked him ONE time, "What did you just say to yourself?" He responded, "I was pretending to the be the president…" I never asked him again what he says. He says he talks to himself because he can't talk back LOL. Well, in this scenario, **I am asking you to argue with yourself. About your days… and also your excuses.**

#5. "**I can't control this**". BS. You are in control of every aspect of your life. That's a hard fact to swallow when there is nothing/no person to blame. I know it's hard, and I have played the blame game. I am for sure a controlling person, but that also makes me very aware of what I cannot control.

***You are** in control of…..*

- Your commission check
- HOW you speak about your business
- How often you talk about your business and to whom
- How many customers you gain
- Your future
- Your reactions
- Your efforts

*You **are NOT** in control of…*

- Your friends and family's perception
- How your customers respond to the products/business
- Your business partners' success or lack of
- The past
- Your competitors
- The weather

This 'not controlling' aspect usually turns into the blame game. "My mentor or upline isn't supportive". **Dude, this is your business. Period.** Excuses are another way of saying obstacles. And obstacles show up just to measure how badly you want something. I had all of the prior excuses present when I was only in this business for fun. But when my Why got serious, and I more than desperately wanted success, I overcame them. *Control what you can, accept what you cannot, and keep moving.*

CHAPTER 6 - KEEP YOUR ATTITUDE IN CHECK:

Had a little attitude in the prior portion. oops. So how about your attitude? What in the world does that mean? Is your attitude in the right place, or at least are you projecting it to be when you are talking about your business?

#1. **HOW YOU SPEAK** when you are talking about your business and/or products, how you physically speak, plays a huge roll in how someone perceives or develops their first impression about you/your business. Remember when that Jenn girl kept calling me? Remember how I went from wanting to ignore her to spending $695 in a matter of minutes? I can't even blame it on the wine. I just remember she was so damn excited about this new stuff she was selling and this company that she had just started working with. I could not tell you one specific thing she said to me, I just knew that she must have been having fun to be able to communicate that excitement through the phone. It wasn't that Valley Girl OMG voice, she was genuinely convincing me with her tone and confidence that I needed to do this. It's true- you have heard it before. **It's not what you say, but how you say it**, or it's how you made that person feel rather than their actual words. She did it. She got me. Thank god.

Karen: "Hey, Heather! How is your new business going?"

Heather: "Hi, Karen, it's going okay. I don't really know what I am doing but it's just a side gig."

VERSES……..

Karen: "Hi, Heather. How is your new business going?"

Heather: "Karen, I love it. I am learning every day but it's easy to learn cause there is so much help. I already love the community and extra money for sure !"

Karen: "Hey- are you still doing that networking thing"

Heather: "Yup!"

VERSES…

Karen:" Hey- are you still doing that networking thing?"

Heather: "Oh yes, love it more each month. The products work, I help people and get paid. Win-win. Will never stop."

When you are talking about your business, look at the people you are conversing with. Smile from ear to ear when you are speaking of what you do. Stand tall. Seriously, don't slouch or turn away or god forbid stare at your phone. Make them want to hear more, not because of what exactly you said, but how you looked when you were speaking. Because you sounded confident, not quiet, and embarrassed. These all will lead to them asking and wanting more information which is exactly what should be your goal with every conversation.

Speaking of conversations, if you're heading into every conversation like, "OK this is weird, how do I mention my business, what do I say, oh this is weird." Your listeners will feel it. You're making it awkward if you feel it's awkward. Become "Casual and Confident" rather than awkward. The more of a big deal you make it the weirder it will be.

Belief will show through in your voice and expressions rather than your details. I am a goofball and pride myself on not knowing it all because I don't have to: I have the best products and business on this planet and that feeling overpowers my words. If someone asks you something and you don't know the answer it is okay to say that! "Hey, you know I am not sure, but I can certainly find out real quick and get back to you!" Also, when you don't portray yourself as knowing it all or being perfect, it shows the other people that they don't have to be perfect either. This is extremely important. What if he or she is secretly considering the business? They need to know that perfection is not expected.

#2. One thing I know for sure is that one of the most important components of being successful is **being positive !!!!!!!!** So many times in business, and life, where I could have blamed, pouted, or quit, I chose to remain positive. I am not even sure where that part of me came from. Pretty sure it was from teaching those growing students. Young human beings that look up to their teachers to learn, yes, but also to emulate an adult who may more present than some parents. Who wants a negative, grumpy, pessimistic teacher? Not one soul on this planet. You shouldn't be teaching anyone anything if you aren't anything BUT positive. I just think **it feels so much better to just be positive.** The fact that you have wifi, or could purchase this book, proves you are already more fortunate than most on this planet.

"Hey, Johnny, you got a "D". Were you absent for the last 9 weeks? Good luck bringing that grade up." *Disclaimer: that was hard to even type that.*

Verses....

"Hey, Johnny, maybe we need to revisit what a thesis statement is. We will try again and nail it this time- I will help."

"Sarah, you don't have your homework. It's a zero. Learn to be responsible".

Verses....

"Sarah, you don't have to be so upset- it's a homework assignment and I can trust that you did it. Let's just try to set up a system so you can remember it next time."

*disclaimer- LOL it's quite evident I taught middle school not high school

See a simple difference? Are you naturally a negative Nancy, or shall we say 'Karen", these days? (Sorry, I couldn't help it). You CAN change this!! And if your business means that much to you- you will. **Retrain your brain**! Start to retrain by noticing 3 positive changes per day. Changes about anything. Maybe the bus was on time, you made an awesome dinner, you met three new people, or you managed to drink a ton of water. Easy. Your brain will start to look for anything positive.

Once you have that down to a daily habit, create a practice of noticing three changes a day that have *a positive effect on people's ability to do business:* Here are three you can implement immediately that work.

*Do you use email or messenger? If you use messenger, never type again. USE YOUR vocal cords and send voice messages from today forward. Simple, yes, but makes a huge difference. It's personal and they can hear you.

*Phone or facetime? Choose facetime when you can with your remote people.

*Make it a point to thank 3 people a day for something. Does not matter if it's via text, online, or in person. Thank people.

By making the effort to recognize the positive effects of business change, you'll retrain your brain to see change as an opportunity for growth.

Some ways I chose to stay positive in my business when many simply throw in the towel...

- You ended up losing a customer... at he/she tried the product with you.
- Your partner quit? Be grateful he/she chose you and better now than wasting more time with that person.
- Sad you are not advancing in title? Be grateful you are even in the business and getting a commission check when most don't even try.
- Not happy about a new product released? Hey, it's a new product. Think of how many others WILL love it?
- Nobody showed at an event you were hosting? At least you had one! Sit down and use that time to reach out to all invited and make connections.

Nobody hopped on my virtual happy hour, but I got nice hair out of it!

#3. **Celebrate those wins**, any and every win! You need to celebrate the smalls because there are ten losses for each win. Did you get 2 new customers this week? Throw a freaking party in your mind. Make a congratulatory post for yourself. It's a big deal- you just secured **two**

entire new markets. **Your two new communities are everyone THEY know**! You tried something new and it was awful? Celebrate! You tried something new! You did a live video and it stunk? Good-your audience now knows you are not perfect!!

#4. Be Positive or Be quiet.

Because of COVID, we are not hosting what we call a "Summit" weekend in NYC. My most favorite weekend of the year with my business. The best part of Summit was being reinvigorated and SURROUNDED by all positive people year after year. The negative white noise that deters people is not present and all present have the long-term vision needed to make it in business.

If you are a negative Nancy or want to complain, or you don't like the way your business is going, or you are slowing down. **PLEASE BE POSITIVE OR BE Quiet.** When you rant, you bring down. We don't need nor want nor benefit from complaining, comparing, or gossiping. I have removed people from team pages due to negativity. It's one of the most basic of life's lessons we learn when we learn how to use words. Nothing nice to say? Don't open your mouth. I honestly don't know how people can stand to be around negative people. What a poor use of energy.

Another No-No in my house of business if you're in my immediate surroundings, is the **NO DRAMA** policy. A little tougher to try and adopt this policy but I suggest it. We are adults. This is not the seventh-grade telephone game where we talk and chatter. No drama. There is too much beneficial business to get a hold of to be wasting time chatting. There is too much good to be done. I IMMEDIATELY interrupt any drama and insist it stops or the partakers are removed from any team interaction. This will only slow down your (P.A.C.E.)

Positive

Attitude

Can

Excel you

WAKE UP.
KICK ASS.
BE KIND.
REPEAT.

#5. Newsflash! It's not about Hope

Remember, writing makes me think before speaking right away, so know this is the third time I have just attempted the following sentence: "I hope my business takes off!" It's not about hope, PEOPLE. It's work!

It's about doing the work even when you don't want to.

It's about meeting new people and expanding your market.

It's about inviting to events/conversations.

It's about sharing stories so find stories that resemble your potentials.

It's about branding yourself with effort in social media

It's NOT about how successful your upline IS or ISN'T

It's not about how much your upline is helping you

It's not even about if your upline is even around

It's not about recruiting one rockstar

It's not about posting a few times on social media

It's not hoping your "turn" or "time" is soon.

It's not about deserving something

It's not about hope

YOU have to make your goals happen by working.

#.6 "I need a kick in the ass!"

I hear this quite a bit when I am checking in on my business partners. The way I handle it is I give them that one love smack, we revisit their why, and then action items. If they don't do the action items, they aren't serious. Time to spend my energy elsewhere.

I am not a punisher. If you need a kick you need a bigger why. You can do what you want with a business, and if you're stuck it's on you. Some people, again, just want the fun money, community, recognition, lots of reasons. There is nothing wrong with that. Those people are just as important to make a large organization.

If you want the 'big time', and you're not doing the work you need to be doing, reset your goals and your why. What if five years from now, five years of working your business day in and day out, you made $27,000 a month. Would you do your output of work today???? Would you bust your tail to get to that point? Bet you would. And you can. Plenty of money out there could be yours.

When people say, *"You deserve this!"* it may sound like flattery but I feel it is rather insulting. Everyone deserves success if THEY EARNED it. The ones that are achieving gigantic milestones are the ones doing the work.

#7. Comparison is a thief of joy!

THE ABSOLUTE WORST thing you can do in this business: COMPARING yourself to others. I can't compare myself to someone who was in corporate America, or already a makeup artist with thousands of followers, or someone who doesn't sleep, or someone who has ten kids. The only person you should be comparing yourself to is YOU!!! Look in the mirror and ask yourself…are you doing all you can do? Did you do more today than you did yesterday? Are you believing in yourself and if you aren't what will you do to change?????

Remember that fear list you had to create? What have you tackled on that list yet? You know what you're capable of. You know if you're doing your best.

You are your power partner. Be accountable. I have been hearing, "Do you have a power partner? Who is your pawer partner?" A power partner is someone you would pair up with to check-in, exchange goals, and hold each other accountable. Which is GREAT, but maybe there are a few on here that are like me. I am my own power partner. How I hold myself accountable:

First, I make a goal board. Yes, I have a corkboard hanging in my bedroom. I have pictures cut out, goals on the whiteboard all there for me to see every morning. This could be something fun you do as a team. Virtually, too, given today's chaos. Set up a zoom and compare goal boards.

Another tactic for myself: I tell my kids when I have a goal in mind. Even if they don't know exactly what my goal even means, they encourage me or keep me in check. Heck, I told them I wanted to be fabulous at 40 and lose weight. For months up until my birthday, I couldn't even eat an Oreo without being screamed at, "Put it down, mom. Fabulous at 40!"

I also do monthly reflections. I write down what worked, what didn't work, and I plan for the next month. I find out what other leaders are doing and I try them. Power partners are an awesome strategy, but ultimately, it's you in the rink alone. It's proven that if you *put your goals* out there to the universe, **you are more accountable if you know people are watching.**

I was doing a training for the field, yes in my shower, and I, at the time, was running for the highest promotion. When you earn this highest promotion with my company, you get this catalog filled with free trips, jewelry, sometimes exercise equipment, lots of goodies to choose from. I was dead set on getting this diamond necklace that all the leaders have. There is only one big diamond in my life and that is on my finger, so why did I want this? It's a conversation piece. People ask about it, which sparks a conversation that could lead to a new prospect. The sole reason why I wanted it- there is no way you can ignore this necklace. In order to hold myself accountable, I made a fake huge necklace out of paper and wore it while I did my live video in the shower. Ok, weird? Maybe. Did it work for me? Yes. Why? I put it out to the 33,000 people who were watching me in my shower. Wearing that paper necklace was my way making sure they all knew my goal. This would only push me harder, knowing the next training I did that I had to be wearing it.

Diamonds are resilient, solid, valuable, attractive, and each unique; sort of how I see this business. And how you should see yourself.

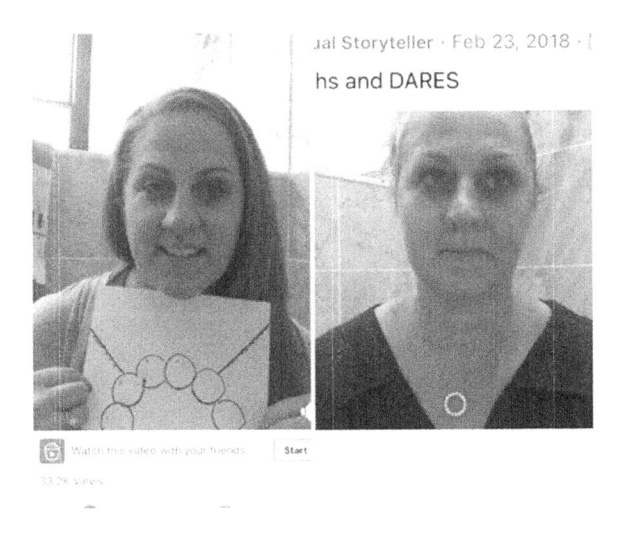

#8. Be Resilient

I was resilient and didn't even know that word existed. The best way I can describe it would be it relates to that phrase, "Put your blinders on". I was in a room at one of our conventions and it was an exclusive invite room where every seat in there was taken by a leader. A corporate big wig was lecturing us and he said, "Every one of you here is resilient. I don't even know all of you, but I know you are resilient cause you are sitting here. To make it to where you are in these seats, the coveted promotion, you have to be." Very simple but very powerful.

I didn't quit when I lost customers. I didn't slow down when a partner strayed or fizzled. I didn't sulk in a bad month. When you commit to a business, you will learn that ALL businesses have surges and pits. I kept moving. Not only because I HAD to, but because I knew what I was striving for was possible. I had the vision. If your vision is in line, you will resist the noise.

CHAPTER 7 - IS YOUR VISION BLURRED?

You have to be able to taste the success, dream about how life would be, and run FOR THAT. That is what gives you the ability to *have* a VISION. Ignoring naysayers, being positive, failing forward...all of this helps when you have a clear vision of *what you want*.

When I was driving what felt like 6,895 thousand miles to work daily, I would truly enjoy my coffee time. Thoughts were processed during my quiet mornings. During MANY of those commuting miles, I would just ponder...., *there has got to be a way for me to make more money*. Then I would shush myself, "Oh Heather, you're a teacher. You can't possibly make much more." And I would think of other things to do. I went and got my real estate license. I ended up having my first son and never initiated a job, but the thoughts were real about wanting MORE.

When I pushed to work harder given the circumstances of moving and job loss, I took a real honest look at the company and what was available. The first realization that I think I could do this came from a reward trip I earned to Napa. Um, hello! Napa- WINE, baby! But what happened was I met normal, real, everyday people just like me. And all different, too, if that makes sense? We all earned this trip. That was inspiring. That, combined with meeting the corporate staff, the doctors, seeing our home office, making lifelong friends, and leaving Napa beyond impressed, my vision was set. I was laser-focused on making it big. I knew by the end of that trip this was it for me.

themselves. "It was an honor and an inspiration," she says. She returned home from the trip with a renewed drive and focus.

Napa trip: red carpet treatment and new friends for life!

So enough of my vision. Time to create yours. I want you to complete something called "fast forward journaling". Yup, homework from the teacher. I want you to put real thought and effort into this Vision writing piece. Think of it as a type of journaling, yes, but in the future writing. Throw yourself into the future one year from today. The typical journaling you are familiar with would have you writing in the present or the past. We are no longer ever thinking in the past from this page forward.

Again, you are going to journal, but journal as though it is <u>one year from now</u>. Take a solid 20 minutes. Put on some relaxing music (I prefer Enya). Write about how your life looks 12 months in the future. Write as if it *already* happened. In your twenty minutes of freewriting, answer the following questions. Again, you want to pretend it is a full year from this day.

Dear Self,

1. How **HAS** your successful business changed your life?
2. Your family's life?
3. Your lifestyle?
4. What is your paid as title/promotion?
5. What is your monthly income?
6. What skills have you mastered that used to be hard?
7. How do you impact your team? Your customers?
8. Who guides you and inspires you?
9. How have you given back?

Now, print it and read it every first day of the month. Or place it on your goal board. Tape it to your forehead. Burn it into your eyes. Imagine this life you can have! IMAGINE that life you *will lead* and go after that vision.

> **The past is your lesson.
> The present is your gift. The future is your motivation.**

CHAPTER 8 - BRANDING YOURSELF

*"You're marketing for the company you're a part of,
but more so for you, SO BE YOU"*

Warning: this might be my favorite part of the book so hang with me. I have so much fun with this on social media, and you should, too. You have such an opportunity to improve your game here, to learn about yourself, and to inspire/impact your audience if you pay close attention to this section.

Some facts to think about before we dive into the art of our language:

1. In the 9 years I have been in this business, Social Media has changed dramatically.
2. Lots of people are selling and sharing via social media making it acceptable to use social media to grow your business.
3. When you take the fact 1 in 6 people have a side gig, side hustle, or second job, it's a fact that there is a ton of opportunity out there. BILLIONS.
4. It's harder to make yourself stand out or, in other words, keep your audience engaging with you. Make them stop their scroll.
5. People can identify the "commercials" a.k.a. boring spamming posts. We don't want that.

social MEdia: then vs now

- It's changed
- It's acceptable to sell
- 1 in 6 currently have a gig
- Harder to stand out and keep audience engaged

> "We don't have a choice on whether we DO social media, **the question is** how well we DO it."
> – Erik Qualman

Soooooo... you need to **Brand Yourself** and learn to *Show not Tell* in your use of social media whether you are dealing with Instagram or Facebook or any platform.

What do I mean by brand yourself? Branding yourself is basically **who you are, or how others perceive YOU** based on what you put out there and share with your social media audience. Let's see if you know who you. Is your brand developing? Is it solid? Or are you scattered everywhere and aren't even sure?

1. TAKE YOUR PENCIL AND PAPER AND DRAW TEN BUBBLES. Bubbles that are large enough for you to write a phrase in.
2. IN EACH BUBBLE write something about yourself. Something that identifies you: a passion, hobby, a favorite anything. WHAT makes YOU, YOU?
3. You must fill in all ten. If you are stuck, ask a BFF, a parent, a partner to describe you as a person *Disclaimer-don't get mad at them they are helping

Here are my bubbles:

Heather Shields/ brand....ME...

- Mom of 3 boys....not just boys, crazy boys
- Wine drinker....box wine drinker

- Positive thinker in every situation and grateful…no question
- Inspirational…try to be… I often think of the underdog
- Dog rescue advocate/dog foster mom
- I love and worship my company
- Funny…perhaps
- Dedicated….
- Good friend
- Good parent but not perfect.

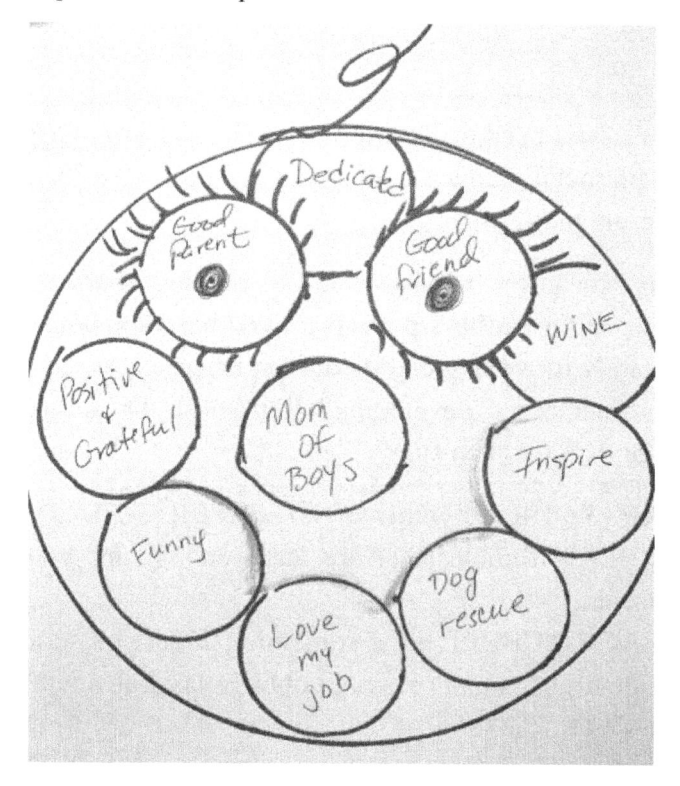

THOSE ARE MY TEN BUBBLES…..EVERY single post or video or whatever I do on social media fills at least one of those categories. If you have to figure out WHO you are, or how you brand yourself, these bubbles should help you focus. Are you portraying these characteristics in your social media? Go look at your social media feed. Scroll three swipes down and peruse just those three pages. Are you a brand when the puzzle pieces fit (you), or are you mish-mash?

A great thing to start doing the second you finish this page; become more aware of your media; what you share and how you share it. Just like you need to think before you speak, think before you post. Is your next share part of your brand- does it align with your bubbles? *Disclaimer- don't drink and post either. Many a morning I deleted.

Branding yourself. Yes, you're selling for a company/brand. That's obvious. Your audience will figure that out. But when you're interacting with social media, and your audience, they want to get to know YOU. So, who are you? Figure it out and develop that. Your audience is not only getting to know you, they'll be interested in what you have to share next, which I the entire point.

You won't see a pristine perfect photo of my three boys dressed up nicely, smiling, or holding hands, with me holding a PTA sign. Nope, not on brand. We don't fit that mold. No pictures of set tables with us saying our prayers- the last dinner post my kids barely had clothes on…but they were all smiles. You can find a selfie of me with an inspirational quote, but you bet my coffee mug has either boobs on it or is something that is somewhat not normal. You will also find me sharing texts from happy clients, rescue dog videos that will make you cry…anything in my realm of bubbles that makes me, ME.

SHOWING not TELLING :

Now you know you need to BRAND who YOU ARE, so let's see if you know how to 'show' rather than 'tell'. Showing NOT telling is an idea I developed from my teaching days. I used to teach 7th grade Language ARTS. THAT WORD "ARTS" has meaning. Writing is an art. To be a good writer, you need to craft in a way that keeps the reader interested. DO you have sentence variety? Is there suspense in your writing? Does your work make the reader want to read on?

To keep your audience interested, you need to keep it interesting... This is also the case when it comes to your crafting of posts. You can do this by **Showing not "Telling"** with your social media.

Here is an example of a favorite writing exercise that I did with my seventh graders every year. I would make them think of a place. They had to use 10 phrases or fun sentences that described this place, but they were not allowed to say the actual name. For example, if they were describing a movie theater, their phrases might be....

"A dark surround with the smell of buttery puffs" (popcorn and darkness)

"Many pairs of eyes glued to one side" (screen)

"A Friday date for many"

"laughs, giggles, and screams can be heard"

"Some scary, some dramatic, some mystery to unfold"

....you get the idea.

They'd present these to the class and the students would have to figure out the place they were describing. Such a fun lesson because the kids were creating and the audience was excited to decode the words and use their brains. Much more interesting then, "A movie theater is a fun place" which is TELLING.

You can relate this to social media also. Anybody can "tell" when it comes to posting. Telling is boring and involves no thought. No thought on the creator's side, and no thought on the audience's side. Here is an example of telling.

You scroll Facebook or Insta and see on someone's page the following post. There is a tube of skincare on the white countertop and text that says, "I love this stuff". That's it. Pretty boring.

Rather than telling, how about you create a post that SHOWS you love this new serum. A much more interesting and thought out post: Place the tube on a floating pillow, in a bubble bath with roses, candlelight, and WINE in the background. Or maybe something more simple like creating a boomerang of you kissing it with bright red lipstick. ('Boomerang' is an ap. Download it and use it to make posts with a little movement in them). Both of the prior examples are much more interesting to show, not tell, the love of a product. The telling post of the box sitting on your counter with boring text won't grab your audience's attention. Nor does it show effort on your attempt at entertainment.

Samples are an integral part of my business: a must, so I often come across many posts. Many. Very. Boring. Posts.

TELLING: "Hey- who wants a sample?" with a picture of the sample.

Why not make it more interesting?

SHOWING: How about your young child in the back seat, holding a sample out the window, and a happily screaming "Only one left -who has not tried this liquid gold?" The audience gets a cute video, gets to see your kid, and you've portrayed that it's urgent as you have one sample left. Where are my fellow dog moms? Try putting a colorful bow tie on your dog, or a hat, and have him with text bubble "Putting on my Sunday best, to deliver the best, to the best- who here needs a treat for your face?"

Last example:

Scenario: My son missed the bus. I am pissed. I immediately want to go to social media and gripe about it. NO! I sit down and look at my brand bubbles …There is no bubble for complaining! People would not expect that from me. INSTEAD, post that having an ADD child can be tough in the morning with making the bus. I SHARE a tip that helps the morning go smoothly, rather than just complain. THAT post is of value, relates to me as a good mom of boys, and it is not negative! *Disclaimer: nobody likes to get on social media and hear complaining. Don't use it as a venting outlet. That would be a great way to lose an audience.*

Impulse post: "UGH- another almost miss for the bus this morning! These boys drive me nuts!"

Filtered through : "Mornings are tough. Especially with some ADD in the morning. A parenting tip that I can share? My kids can pick their breakfast if they get out of bed with the first "Good morning". That, and Nutella waffles, have saved us many mornings!"

The filtered post=positive, crazy boys, parenting advice, real

This little BUBBLE exercise should force you to figure out what makes you, you. Focusing on those characteristics /interests/ traits …whatever is in your bubble chart… will help your audience get to know you. They will get to know you and be back for more. And in doing so, they will also be exposed to whatever you are selling (sharing). But the exposure is not "Hey- look what I am selling? Want to buy some?" It's not a commercial.

"Heather, I buy from you because you aren't an annoying commercial. I love your posts and can tell you love your job. I want to support that."

"You're real on social media. But you're also entertaining and I always look for your next post."

I have heard the previous two compliments more than a few times. And they have been my most favorite of all. Think of this as a posting process filter. Ask yourself these questions while creating social media. Does my post hit on at least one of my bubbles? And, is my post *showing or telling* my audience?

- Check this post out. This momma nailed *showing not telling* here. Cali wanted to illustrate how her products removed makeup. I would say covering her belly with sharpie, then using the products, was a brilliant idea. We SEE the products in action, we learn about her, and I will be checking her page daily to see when those twins come out. 'A' for effort, 'A' for uniqueness, 'A' for demonstrating , freaking 'As' all over that post.

> *Disclaimer- I did not know how to add a sticker, so I drew one myself! No time to waste when you got goals booo-yah!!!*

Partner up with someone who is in the same company, or a power partner, and help each other post check. "Hey, if I do this, is this enough showing or is it telling?" Or, "Shanaynay, send me your next 5 post ideas before hitting that button so we can work on making them more showing!"

Telling
Help brand you?
Interesting?
Not showing
Keep interesting

Are you able to be vulnerable?

One of your bubbles might be something that is normally kept private to most. I say you should think about sharing that part of your life and put yourself out there. When you do this, people trust you. This is not easy for everyone. But when you do this, you open yourself up to connecting with a whole new community of people.

Recently, I had breast reduction surgery. The night before surgery, I sat in my shower and went live. On my public page! All I said was this is what I am doing, I am a little nervous, I might be quiet for a while, and would appreciate kind prayers. It was a last-minute decision and the response was remarkable. Not only did people come out of the woodwork that I had forgotten about, but many came forward who had already gotten the surgery and gave me advice. WIN-WIN on so many levels. I wanted to keep this private until I realized it was an opportunity to be real, be unique, and grow my network.

I joined three social media groups that were breast reduction focused.

I put my surgical journey out there, shared tips with the world and started to gain a whole new Following of friends. I made a LONG live video where I suggested products that helped my healing. I described the recovery process and gave my recommendations on what clothes to have on hand. That video, one year later, is *still* being viewed which constantly connects me to new people.

Make yourself stand out by showcasing who you are. You are unique.

I am not a supermodel. I don't wear fabulous clothes. I am not a genius, but I am real......and I believe people feel that.

When we were on a reward trip to Hawaii, it was our first huge trip as a couple, I remember being in the conference room. Everyone in there was a top earner. My husband and I sat between a secretary and a doctor. The secretary, myself, and the doctor were all at the same level in the company. Different ages, different personalities, and a variety of education levels *sitting at the same table*, all in the same earning income bracket.

THE BEST part about any network marketing business opportunity is that is there for anyone. Does not matter your age, ethnicity, gender, past, doesn't matter your degree or lack of degrees. I taught smelly 7th graders Language arts.

So, Be Real by **BEing YOU**

Many people refer to Facebook as "Fakebook" and I get why. We see the perfect vacations, the smiling family photos, the head to toe on brand first day of school photos, the pictures of cute faces. When we don't always fit the expected Fakebook and show our realness, you stand out. Everyone is unique, so let's get back to being ourselves.

STRAIGHT TALK FROM THE SHOWER GIRL

Social MEdia

*Brand **YOU**rself

*Show **NO**t tell

*Be vulner**ABLE**

***BE** a billboard

BE a billboard

PROMOTE yourself — YOU ARE YOUR OWN BRAND

CHAPTER 9 - RECRUITING FOR LONGEVITY

Some people cringe when they hear the word "recruiting". When I hear it, I think of longevity, sustaining a business, necessary, challenging, new friendships, and giving a GIFT ...so much greatness.

I am going to start with the most important here, in my opinion, when it comes to recruiting. Have the **"This is a Gift Mindset".** If you have "the gift mindset", everything else, when it comes to recruiting, will be easier.

The most important thing to realize and remember is that each time you expose someone to your opportunity you're doing them a favor! Take a look at the following list. A *close* look...

- Keeping my family fed and housed while my husband is out of work
- Paying for TWO private high school tuition payments! It feels amazing!
- Unpaid maternity leave. Every little bit helps
- Student loan payment ☹
- Paid my daughter's dance tuition for the year

- Able to stay home with my children
- My biz has paid for my full investment out of pocket to open my own salon!
- This year alone with my commission only I've paid off ~75% of my debt!
- I'm getting a new computer 🖥 and next month, for my son
- Last week my cat had to go to the vet emergency room, so I had to pay the vet bill, medicine, and special food. This money is a blessing because I can replenish what I had to pay to care for him.
- I'm paying for our lake house next week! Feels good to be able to pay for it myself without asking my husband
- I am making a donation to Feed America and the rest of the money pays for my daughter's horse 🖤
- Paying for IVF treatment
- I was able to pay all the bills for the next month. That extra helps a lot!

The above list is a quick look at what people are doing with their commission checks from their direct selling businesses. Whatever company you are with, you have the opportunity to help someone earn extra income. That money can be of huge importance to people! Donations, vet bills, computers, making up for lost income, helping GROW YOUR FAMILY …those are big deals! All because someone asked them to learn about an opportunity.

One day someone said to me, "**You just sell skincare**". Ummm yeah, I got a 'lil fired up. They were ill-informed about all that we, and others, do. To anyone who may think this is nothing more than fancy face creams, our businesses are so much more. When people earn extra money, it changes their lives, large and small. When you support a small business owner, rather than big box stores, this is what you are supporting.

IMAGINE if the people below **were never GIFTED an Opportunity!**

*A nurse and police officer, married and now retired, just finished building a 147-acre farm, dog training facility, and place for wedding ceremonies that will employ children with special needs. A dream of theirs their previous professions could never fund.

*A mom that I traveled to Hawaii with now funds surgeries for children who can gain their vision back.

*Another mom funds surgeries for kids with cleft pallets.

*Building a Schools and orphanages in Africa

"I got to quit cleaning houses after 18 yrs of doing so"

*I get to donate more to charities close to my ♥☐!

*I have a whole new tribe of friends and a wonderful feeling of self-accomplishment!

*I'm paying for someone to build a well for a Cambodian family to drink FRESHWATER for the rest of their lives.

*It's enabled my kids to go to a better school!

*It paid for our mortgage when my husband lost his job unexpectedly!! and It's enabled us to sponsor a child from Africa!

*It saved us from losing our home.

*It gave me the chance to follow the thing that's nearest and dearest to my heart: philanthropy! Which in turn has affected how we are raising our kids

*The financial burden of being a single income family is removed from my husband.

*I give my full paycheck to my church.

*It's allowed me to survive when child support suddenly stopped and I had to be a single mom

*After being a stay at home mom for 3 years I was feeling inadequate by not financially assisting our home.

*Being a disabled Veteran, it has proven impossible to hold a normal job because I could have debilitating migraines that would come out of nowhere and stay for days on end. This not only rendered me unable to work, but it also robbed me of feeling like I was useful. RF has given me back something I never thought I would have again: the ability to provide for my boys above and beyond the restrictions of a disability check and a piece of me I never thought I would have again.

*After going through breast cancer, I was lost. I didn't feel like a woman and felt like I was weak and incapable. I had never felt that before. This business made me feel powerful, beautiful, and strong again and gave me something of my own again outside of being a mom, wife, and admin. It has given me back to ME!

*A mom of 7: ... has given me the ability to show my girls that mommies can have it all. Work and a successful business and be a mom full time. I don't have to miss a minute.

*.... has given me the ability to change others' futures too by growing my team. There's nothing better than getting a text on Payday saying "THANK YOU!"

*.... is helping my husband and I further fertility treatments. (we now have one baby boy and another team member who is 20 weeks prego!)

To the consultants in any network marketing company, keep on with your bad self because you have chosen a great avenue for revenue. From paying rent to contributing, to giving, to HECK, making babies, you have a gift to offer. That is your one job- do not withhold this gift from anyone. Below is an actual letter I wrote to my team on New Years….pretty much sums it up.

Your ONE job…….

Dear Team Why Inc.,2018.

Thank you is not enough. You, every single one of you on this team, is the best gift of 2018.

Handing over my retirement letter from teaching was the hardest thing I have ever had to do- because the people I worked with were my family. I was afraid to leave that family. I had NO idea that there was an even better family out there.

I have more friends now, at 41, than I ever have. I have more support in my life NOW, than I ever have. I have more encouragement, now, than I ever have. I have met wonderful and continue to meet new wonderful people all of the time NOW because of this company… and I will always have this choice- to meet new people. Which I love. And to meet GOOD people who are always giving is the best thing right NOW in such a tough world. I am part of the BEST, NOW, because someone told me about it.

I used to wake up early in the morning, on purpose, and leave my three babies so they wouldn't see me. Then I would get home, be busy with schoolwork, they'd be tired, and they'd be in bed three hours after I picked them up. NOW, because I don't have to have a 9-5, I am ALWAYS with them. I make their lunches instead of wondering what they ate. I drive them if they miss the bus because a shoe was lost, and I know this helped make their day better. I drive them to sports, to playdates, we bring friends everywhere- there are always people here with US- instead of me being absent and stressed

In the past, I have been in the grocery line with my kids climbing out of the cart, not sure if my debit card would clear. This was all while working my ass off as a teacher…it wasn't enough and probably would never be. Now, I get a kick out of paying for peoples' groceries - or giving whenever I want. Being able to give WHENEVER I want NOW because someone decided to tell me about this...

So, the best gift (besides my kids obv) I have ever received, has been this business. I hope you can offer this, and so much more, to yourself and everyone. As cheesy as it may sound or fru fru, you - this team- really has made me who I am, happy with my daily get up, inspire me to do more, and be more, and have made me want to be better.

Please know there is no me without you!

Imagine if someone decided not to talk to me because they were nervous or was afraid to say the wrong thing or didn't think I needed this! Don't take this away from someone- you don't know! You might be holding the gift the person next to you needs. So go !!!!! Go now, go fast, go hard!

If you DON'T, Someone else WILL

This is quite simple and a FACT. I can promise you that. If you don't ask everyone you know and get to know in the future, to join you in business, someone else WILL ASK THEM. This is a hard lesson to learn and I lived it. It blows. No other phrase better to describe it.

I have a close friend that is what we call a 'sideline sister'. We do not have a vested interest in each other in a business sense as we are not on the same team, but she's a great friend. Her name is Melissa. Ohhhhhhhh Melissa reminds me all of the time that she learned this lesson….

I have a Rockstar, no other better way to describe her, on my team who is currently earning her free car. She's very successful as that rolling trophy is significant. Her name is Marcy. Marcy is brilliant, dedicated, and she works like no other I have ever seen. Marcy had a why and a vision from day one. *#belikemarcy*Well, one day I posted about Marcy and how she had qualified for all of these amazing trips, and how much of a worker she is. Yup- you guessed it. Marcy and

Melissa grew up together. Melissa never thought to ask Marcy. Oooooops.

That's Melissa in the first picture. I still have goals and one is to be as successful as her! The second picture is me and Marcy. See how tight my grip is on her?

You better adopt that gift mindset and start asking!

Become a Pro, then find them

There are three types of recruits you will find. And you will if you are growing a team and duplicating that. Marcy, myself, and Melissa are Pros☺.

Posers. Agh, posers. Not going to lie- I was a poser, at first. Posers think they will recruit a few and hope to win the lottery with one of them. Find that gold nugget and cash it in! Doesn't work that way in this beautiful business or any that I know of. When I recruited that doctor's office, you know, the fat doctor where I gave blood for a conversation? When they joined, I literally started looking at free cars and thought I hit the lottery. He never sold a thing. You don't sit pretty boxes on a counter and expect people to buy them. I went to poser rehab I guess.

Next, are Amateurs. Amateurs have a Poser mindset but also worry and look for shortcuts. They sound like a whole lot of work and negativity. I am glad I jumped to the Pro category.

Pros become an expert at the skills required to build a large and successful organization. And then they duplicate that down. So, ask yourself which are you? How would your mentor see you and which of the three would you want on your team? You need to recruit and recruit many to find the pros. You have to become one first, though. And remember to love the posers and amateurs on the way. You never know when their WHY might change. #winkwink

10 and 2: a SIMPLE calculation

I have never been good at math. I never liked any math class. But I do remember one class. I remember, in tenth grade, my math teacher saying to me, in front of the entire class, "Heather, you are the reason parents get divorced." Now, granted, he was joking. Pretty sure I was talking while he was teaching. Imagine that. I did break the rules, but there is a line you don't cross. To say something like that to a young person, in front of peers, with no idea about her life, as a joke? I, in my heart, believe it is one of the reasons I wanted to teach kids. I would at least know that for the years that I taught, the hundreds of students in my room, for a few hours a day, would be cherished, praised, and loved. Never a day like that would be had.

Disclaimer-OK that was leaning towards what should be a session with Margaret LOL. You have to laugh, people. Laugh and get a therapist.

Simple math is what I was starting to write about. It's all about duplication. I wish I had been introduced to this concept early in my journey before reading it in a book. I wish I would have also taught it to my team earlier- or duplicated it- because it is all about simple duplication.

The 10/2 rule as I understand it. *Disclaimer- remember this is my unique story.* Gain 10 customers. Recruit 2 of those customers to join your business. Train those 2 who joined to get 10 customers. Have 2 of those 10 customers also join. Keep teaching. You, as a teacher will benefit from all of the **duplicating**. It's such a simple concept. Anyone can truly get 10 customers if they tried. 2 of those will want something MORE so find out what that MORE is. Take a peek at my non-professional graphic illustration below. You are the big blue. You acquired ten clients. Two of your clients became reps. Those reps each gained ten customers and so on. Simple math, doable duplication, residual income, deep, if the pattern continued.

10 and 2: you can do

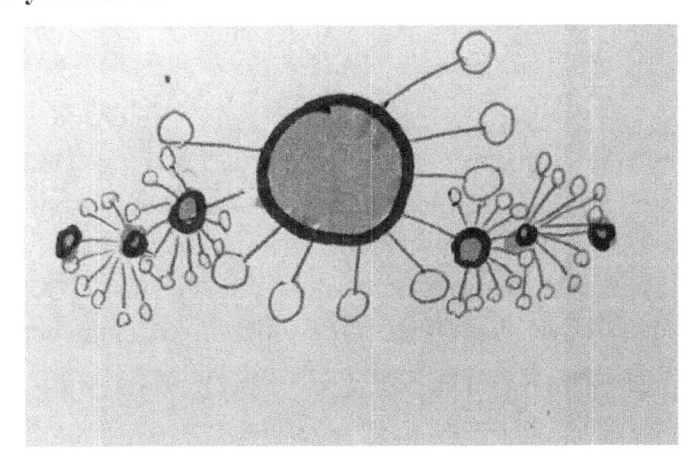

TINY- it's a big deal

Let's be honest, nobody likes small things. Especially when it comes to 'reasons'. Have you ever heard of this 'T.I.N.Y." though? Their Interest Not Yours? Who is 'their'? Anyone who you are discussing a business opportunity with.

When you are speaking to someone about any business, or even just a live conversation, you want to find out 1. What are their interests? 2. Are they lacking in anything? 3. What would they love???? OK, that is a lot. So.......you take this "find out their interests" and plug into that. Your business could help with "that". It's never about what someone can do for you. Ever. Do they mention being bored? Maybe they are looking for challenges. Are they complaining about long work hours? Maybe adding another stream of income could eventually let them cut back. Do they love their job but miss the collaboration or recognition? Show them what your business offers! This could be a fit for them, but you will never find out unless you ASK and LISTEN for *Their Interests Not Yours*. It's a *big* deal to them, so find out what they want or need or are missing in their life.

OR

One of my most favorite people on earth, Myisha, (she's as awesome as her name is) showed me a new SIMPLE tactic you can use if the above was too heavy for you. Ask *this simple* question, "Are you happy?" Three words. Anyone can ask. Anyone can answer. It's the answer you listen to and take it from there. "Are you happy?"

Why are they not happy? Lacking friends? Want to contribute? All their possible 'WHYs' are right there in that answer. So, simply ASK. But you have to follow up with the listening part which is hard when you are or should be, very excited about your business. Do not vomit your company all over them. Listen. Absorb. Continue the conversation, connect with people, and start forming relationships.

CHAPTER 10 - SIMPLE WHY

Perhaps you have been in business for some time already and are rebooting yourself. Forget how to recruit? I think I did. Or maybe you are brand new (and very smart for already reading this book), and ready to run with this. Regardless of where in your journey, when you are talking to people remember WHY you started (or are starting).

I for sure lost sight of this. I am sure many eyes were rolled when I was talking about a free car or trips to France and diamond necklaces. I would, too! But I forgot to keep it simple. People can't think that large in the beginning because it seems so out of reach. What people probably can relate to is needing or benefitting from another $300 or so a month! Which is doable in any business. FACTS, as my son would say.

When your newbies join, earn that extra income, see what is possible AND available to earn, *then* you reach for the big time. Don't start that way. Start simple, and realistic. If Jenn called me up and said, "Hey, Heather. You can earn a car and trips to Spain and France and make a crap ton of money working from where and whenever you want!" I would have spit out my Shiraz. By the time I saw all of those tangible pots of gold, I was already invested for life.

CHAPTER 11 - NEVER QUIT

The only losers are quitters in this industry. Keep going. What's the saying, "It's a marathon, not a sprint"? I ran the Marine Corps marathon right after 9/11. Yes, that 9/11. I trained for a grueling 7 months, so what I say below I can say with experience. My journey can surely accurately be compared to a marathon.

Marathons are hard as hell.

Be prepared to get up when you fall. Be prepared to practice eating certain foods- some may not work well on long runs. Be prepared to shit yourself. You will be surrounded by people who drop like flies, and you will want to collapse.

Keep going.

Your legs will cramp and ache like they want to rip away from your body, but when you reach that next mile marker you will forget the pain. When you hydrate and fill yourself up with all things good, you will gain the strength to keep going.

Fill up.

Find others who are training and plan runs together. A like-minded company is always a bonus. Always train in all types of weather, as the future days are unpredictable. You might enter a storm and will have needed the rain running practice. When the supporters offer you water and oranges do not pass them up.

Don't stop. Ever.

When you have crossed that finish line and your ultimate goal, do not stop. Do not stop moving your legs. You'll eventually find yourself right at the start line again if you do.

All in the head

You don't just decide one day you're going to run 26.2 miles and go the next week. You suffer and enjoy the journey all at the same time. We all are built the same way: skeletal system, muscles, brains (some more than others- sorry), hearts...I will stop there. It's those who can overcome the mental part who cross that finish line.

I would say for about the past 9 months, at least 2 or 3 times per month, I would open up my inbox and see messages like the following:

"Hey, my girl quite and I need the lash stuff like yesterday. Can I order from you?"

"Hi, Heather. I see you are a consultant. My old girl has not been getting back to me- I think she quit. Am I able to get my products from you?"

And I would have no problem taking care of those abandoned customers, of course, after I made sure their prior consultants were no longer active (karma). And I will happily take over their networks the quitters now lost, and then those networks and so on. A duplication I enjoy- they should never have quit. It's literally like throwing money out the window.

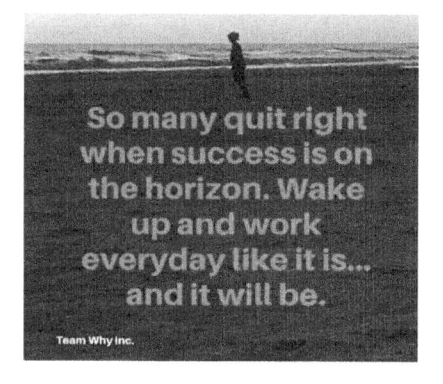

> So many quit right when success is on the horizon. Wake up and work everyday like it is... and it will be.
>
> Team Why Inc.

CHAPTER 12 - LEADING: NO TITLE NEEDED

If you don't quit, you're already a leader and, most likely, have some people to guide. If you don't YET, lead yourself, chin up, until you find your team that is already out there waiting.

If you have, or are building, a team there are few qualities I believe are important when it comes to guiding others. There are lots, but we all are different and we all can decide for ourselves how we lead best, but I wanted to make sure I gave you my input as you do this in your journey.

First of all, if you have one person as a partner, guess what? You are a leader. If your company has titles or promotions or advancements or levels, **DO NOT wait** to be a certain "level, stature, title, promotion," to feel like you can't label yourself as a leader. No position anywhere can identify someone as a leader. The community doing the following decide who will lead them. Lead now, lead with integrity, and lead by example.

I had the itch to get up in front of a crowd, grab my projector, and run a business presentation. *Noooo, I have to be this coveted five in order to do so* I thought. Says who? Someone must have because that is was I thought. Wrong. Man, I wasted some important months for sure those years ago.

Although you are a leader, please **do not be a micromanager**. 9 years in, I can tell you if I could get back the number of hours I put into trying to "manage" people I would. And on the flip side, there is nothing worse than being given a task, working on it, then having all of your work shunned because the task giver did it themselves.

You might be a micromanager if these thoughts run through your head...

"It will be faster and easier if I just do it myself."

"I can't let anything go wrong."

"They need me- or they are going to mess up."

"They won't get it done and I will look foolish."

On the flip side, your team is feeling....

"She's doing it because she doesn't trust us."

"We won't live up to her expectations."

"She's perfect. We can't ever be."

Put your red pen away and let your team learn and grow. You are demoralizing them in the long term, and debilitating yourself along the way. You want to make leaders who then make leaders. You don't want people to always have to depend on you. Teach them and set them free...oh it is a glorious thing when your superstars don't even check in LOL. Remember, we want people to fail forward. If you aren't letting them fail, they ain't moving anywhere but probably away from you.

If they are asking, they are working!

Very simple concept here. You will have people who will join you in business, and then you will never hear from them again. They ghost you from day one or do a little and disappear. Strange, but it is not our job to try and figure out people. You will also come across people who contact you a gazillion times a day. But if you have worker bees that are reaching out with questions, that means they are working.

I have a young crazy smart superstar on my team who is just a walking ray of light. I still chuckle when I think about those first few weeks right after she joined me. My boys and I would be in the car and my phone would go off like 10 to 15 times in a row. The kind of text notifications that one might get from young people- like rapid-fire shots. It was almost like the never-ending rapid gunfire. My middle son would always pick up the phone and hand it to me, "Mom, Laura needs something." It became a normal nature…always texting, always asking, always conversations.

Then it slowed.

She gained her confidence and leader wings.

And was off. I missed the constant communication but she quickly learned and found her way. And once something was taught, it was never addressed again. So, work with the working, and soon they'll be working on their own. You can then spend your time finding the other worker bees.

Recruiting is simply signing someone up. Sponsoring is when you commit to them. You're WILLING to help them and teach them. It is our responsibility as a sponsor to teach them how to grow their business and duplicate down IF THEY HAVE THE DESIRE and are coachable. Lead them when they ask.

The Others' Reflections

I am sure you have heard, "Stop doing…start doing…keep doing." It's important to self- reflect and ask yourself these questions for sure- I would say at the end of every month. Make it a habit. But It's almost more important to ask other leaders this same question.

Women are naturally dramatic. That is why to THIS DAY, I am flabbergasted by the comradery I have been surrounded by. We have about 20, all at the same level, who have been working together for the past 9 years. But- there is no real personal gain when it comes to profiting from each other. I think we are all just smart enough to know that collaboration works. 20 great minds, minds that all felt we **WERE MADE FOR MORE**, are better than one standing alone. So, at the end of every month, you have 20 smarties sitting around sharing all of the ideas and regrets and inspiration and slip-ups- you learn a lot and you expand your experience vicariously through other leaders. It sure helps your journey.

The best way to lead?

By far, the best way to lead is by doing. DO what you ask your team to do. Show them that you are in the trenches with them.

If you are sharing the top numbers of your teams monthly (like posting the top 20 on a team page), and you are not in the top, oh boy- they see you...That is not the kind of duplication you want to see happening. Get back up there.

If you are telling your team to host events, in person or virtually, or any kind, you better be doing them yourself.

If you want to inspire your team, do so by reaching your own goals, that, of course, you had shared with them. And if you don't reach them, you are also showing them you are not perfect. But they saw you **DO** your best, right?

CHAPTER 13 - LEARN FROM MY MISTAKES AND SHARE YOURS

In doing your best, mistakes were surely made. Gosh, I made so many, so how did I have such success? Again, I did enough failing to move forward. I tried enough new things that I learned some did not work for me. If you're comfortable doing the same things over and over, you'll eventually stall.

You Can't DO this FOR People

'Tiz was a doozy I wish I had learned sooner in my journey to a million. *Disclaimer- it is still surreal writing that $ phrase.* Helping people makes me happy. Naturally then, when I go to help someone and then that person does not flourish, I get down on myself. I took one instance so personally that it angered me and I had to figure out why. This is where I learned it's not my job to DO the work.

I had a friend join me for the sole purpose she needed $800 a month to keep her house during a pretty bitter divorce. In my mind, I am thinking this is completely doable. And she is coachable, which means she will get to this goal. Wrong. I put more effort in it than she did. When she quit after hardly even starting, I was livid. What a waste of energy. I learned there that you *can not DO this FOR people*. You should help them get started, encourage them along the way, be there but in the end, it is their job and the numbers that come out on that commission check have no correlation to your efforts.

100% chance you will end up in business with a friend or family member, so one of the hardest aspects to accept is that **THIS *IS* A BUSINESS.** You HAVE to separate emotions. You have to accept that there will be conversations- tough ones. You have to accept that some may not take it as seriously as you. And that's okay. The last time I checked, women are naturally emotional, much more so than men. In my industry, it is more lady based so this could be a wall you face. *Never lead with your emotions.*

The best two pieces of advice I can give, because I DID NOT do them in the beginning, is never to answer or respond to someone who has angered you right away. Go for a walk, or at least count to ten before you even think of replying. I like to type out an immediate response and delete it, take some breaths, and then retype when my head is not raging. To be a successful entrepreneur, you must navigate away from your feelings. It's not personal- it's business. If you don't those who have learned to steer clear of the emotional path will pass you up as you spend the time mending bridges and addressing drama when you could be taking orders, recruiting others, and helping.

Speaking of business, **lead with it**! A HUGE mistake I made for about the first year, was trying to get the products first into peoples' hands. Now I know I should have got the BUSINESS in their life first. I did know better, but it makes sense now that I am a gramma in the business. If I can offer amazing products to people, and someone wants them, then you want them to try and get their market to want them, too. Everyone benefits. There is no awkward feeling when you WANT a customer on your team after he or she orders for a year- you've already planted the seed on day one.

A Welcomed third wheel

"I have got this."

"They don't want to hear from a stranger."

"They trust me- I don't need a partner call."

…ever said those to yourself? I did.

Wrong.

Wrong.

… and Wrong.

Third-party validation is a tool, that if available for you, you should use. I didn't understand what third party validation was in the beginning, let alone how crucial it is in this type of business.

You don't have to do this alone. If people in your company are willing to help, take the help. Even if you have what you think is a stinky upline, find one that you align with and ask for help. They are out there. Another leader may have a better answer to a question than you. Another person might have a similar situation to your prospect- meaning they will relate to each other better. They already know you, they may want to hear someone else's point of view. I LOVE "Three-way calls" or "Business chats", whatever you prefer to call them, and would love if they happened daily. From the third party's point of view, I found that the prospects on the calls were more inclined to ask ME the harder questions rather than the person or friend bringing the call. They couldn't offend me because they didn't know me.

It's also a GREAT way to get to know your team members early on if you are the leader on the call. WHEN they join your company and team, you already know their voice. You've already communicated and, therefore, know each other at least a little.

It's a fast way to duplicate and grow. All three parties learn on those calls, or zooms, or coffee meetings. At first, fair warning, you will be nervous running them. And probably horrible the first few times. But you'll soon see how effective they can be. I remember I would talk and talk and talk and talk to the point where I got annoyed if I had to tell my story one more time. And these people didn't hop on a call to listen to me yap. An intro and snapshot of yourself is great, but those conversations are for Q&A and getting to a close.

I have locked myself in closets so I could take a call. I have hidden in the car to take a call. I have sat outside in the snow during a Christmas party to answer the phone. My close friend now, whom I met on our Hawaii trip, was on a call and FELL backward off her chair, jumped right back up mid-sentence, and continued. Another friend would pump and nurse during that trip WHILE on a call. We knew, at that point, how critical- in a positive way- they can be to grow your business. *Just Say Yes to Three Ways (*calls lol).

Have NO Expectations

Kind of sounds weird, huh? But it's a simple, sound, crucial piece of advice here. Have no expectations, on so many levels. I was horrible with many judgments which forced me to learn *not to have ANY expectations.* It truly keeps you from disappointments. Let me show you...

I girl from my high school called me up a few years after I started my business and said, "Okay, I am sick of just watching you all. Want to meet for coffee?" OF COURSE. She had seen the team grow and grow with many from our high school. We love getting those kinds of messages, right? When they reach out to us? Usually, they are very smart people and she was.

So we met. We had coffee, we talked, and she wanted some extra money for a couch. Recently divorced, two adorable kids, lived close by, and she hated people. Yes. She sat in the coffee shop and literally said, "I want to do this but there is one problem though. I hate people." I left the store and called my mentor. I said, "Jenn, you can have her- she hates people." I thought there was no way she could do networking while hating people.

She joined, I helped her launch, I helped her launch 2 of her new directs. I guided her like I guided all of my newbies and she took off. She made it to the coveted level where she could certainly buy more than a couch.

I expected her to not do well as I assumed people who don't like people would struggle. She learned and had a strong network. And, she is a nurse; nurses are smart, liked, trusted, and underappreciated. I did not expect someone who does not like people to even have an interest in networking. I did not expect her to do so well.

I also expected my best friend for life to jump aboard with me. Didn't happen.

My best friend from college did and that was COMPLETELY unexpected☺. She expected her family to be supportive and at least buy products. Didn't happen. A Rockstar on my team who I thought was a 'lifer' with our company doesn't even work the business anymore- after earning so much and so many trips. I expected her to be around forever. And she's gone.

At a Halloween bonfire, an acquaintance of mine mocked me when someone else asked when my next reward trip was. She chimes in, "Oh my gosh -if I hear one more thing or see one more post about your products and business blah blah blah blah." Unexpected, besides rude. I was so caught off guard I just took a swig of beer to keep my lips closed. One week later at our school Halloween fundraiser, I donated a huge basket of my company's products for the silent auction. I did not expect Karen to be the one with the highest cash offer and win☺. Yes, the lady who was mocking me. Now her AND her mother are re-ordering clients under someone on my team here. Oh, the irony. I slept well that night.

I expected my business to suffer when I was recovering from surgery, which took months, from a breast reduction. It actually thrived. I expected my first clients to move on to other products after supporting me for so long. They haven't. I expected after a few years I would get bored. No way. I did expect to make money, I mean who would do this, otherwise. I did not, however, expect- let alone dream of- making well over a million and counting.

CHAPTER 14 - MONEY- ARE YOU THINKING 'BIG PICTURE'?

FACTs: *Money is important.* People join businesses, start businesses, look for side gigs, change jobs, or work two jobs FOR MONEY. We can say, "It's not for the money" and sound real peachy and politically correct. But that would be deceiving. It is for the money. It's for WHAT THE MONEY is GETTING YOU!

More time home instead of t your 9-5?

Drop overtime hours?

Summer camp for your sanity?

Contribute to the home?

A Louis Vuitton?

Save money for college?

Pay off debt?

> "Money doesn't matter," said nobody EVER!
>
> Team Why Inc.

Those all take money. Not rocket science there. So, yes, money plays a role. Money also decreases stress, helps others, and is a necessity for living.

Let's look at some supposed monthly commission checks. Monthly, then a few months out, one year, then years…..to the big picture of ten years out let's say. I am officially working on ten years myself in the industry. Everything today is so 'Instant' and 'right now' that people lose sight of looking forward -in any sense.

Your checks are $250 a month = $3,000 a year. Could that be a family vacation? College savings? That would be $30,000 in ten years if your commissions were consistently $250 a month.

You get $350 a month = $4,200 per year = $42,000 for ten years.

$450 commission check per month= $5,400 for one year and that being $54,000 over ten years

$600 a month gets you $7,200 a year / $72,000 for ten years

$750 a month = $9,000 and $90,000 for ten years

$1,000 obviously is 12,000 a year, $120,000 for ten years (*Disclaimer- damn)

$1,100 =====$13,200 Ten years of that $130,200 is EASILY college

Look at what you are earning or want you WANT to earn! And think past tomorrow.

(Again, this is my unique story). My first pay was $357. If I was happy with those commissions and remained ONLY wanting that Target fun money, that puts me at $4,284 for the year. So me being 9 years in, I would today have made $38,556. That is real money! Even if you increase your commission checks $100 more each month for the first year (357,457,557....), you'd be at $9,929 instead of $4,284 for the first year alone let alone 9 years out. *Disclaimer- that was some common core math.* Hopefully, you get my point.

If you want to make your commission checks grow...

- Get customers
- Get business partners
- Have your business partners get customers

And have your business partners get partners to do the same (The 10 and 2 simple duplications).

How do I track?

I look for 10% growth every month ...Whether you are a team of 1, or 10, or 100, or 1000, shoot for a ten percent increase minimum per month. I am not a math person, but if you have a friend named Siri she can even do the math for you.

CHAPTER 15 - NETWORKING...

THE ONLY CONSTANT

"I don't know enough people" or "Everyone knows I am doing this": two statements I hear quite a bit. And I totally get it. But the truth is we are constantly meeting people. Whether in person or online, the ways to increase the number of people in your network are plentiful.

If you are in a networking business, networking itself has to take a priority or you may feel tapped out. So, are you honestly making networking itself a priority? A daily priority? Me being 9 years in, this is tough for me. It's tough for many. Let's be honest about how much we are or are not networking. Right now may be different given the 2020 circus year it's been. The COVID world makes this all the more difficult for sure. So, yes, times have and are changing. We still need to network and the ways to connect with people, and in turn, THEIR network will always exist as long as we have the internet.

My blood type is my business. I live it, breathe it, admittingly obsessed with it. How can I not be when it's had this much of an impact on my life? The VERY FIRST thing that pops into my head when I am in a new situation or given an opportunity to be around people, or something new, I ask myself, "Okay, how can this get me to know people and slip in my business if the chance arises?" I am CONSTANTLY thinking this way. Half of the time, **you already are**

networking. You just need to make your business more a part of your blood and think outside of the box.

No, I am not viewed as "The perfume sprayer"! You know the one that walks in the room and everyone runs away from? No, I don't go up to people and say, "Hi, nice to meet you. Are you currently happy with your skincare routine?" Ummmmmmm, no thank -you. You can be tactical and smart and NOT be annoying. Networking means connecting and meeting new people- not throw up your business on them minute one. Take a look at some of my favorite examples from myself or the team.

My Rockstar Marcy, you know the one Melissa never approached, her business is also her blood type. Her son had a math project where a model needed to be constructed as a portion of the project. Her son built an eye cream from our company for his project. Brilliant. I mean it legit looked like a jar of eye cream that was the size of a keg! I would have purchased it myself if it were real. Guess who is a client of Marcy's now? Her son's math teacher who got to learn all about our products. And, he got an 'A'.

I was addicted to Spin class. When we had them. I decided one day to donate to one of the classes. A free tanner- everyone wants to be tan. So, I gave it to the teacher to raffle off during an always filled Saturday morning class. How convenient. It was up to the teacher to decide how the winner would earn it. So there's that- 28 bikes filled with people who now know what I sell. "OK, we have a giveaway here so generously from Heather… whoever hits 3 miles the fastest, go!" she screams in a room where nobody could ignore that.

I have the most unique looking dog you will ever see. Trust me. He was just in the middle of training classes to become a therapy dog before the COVID days. What a way to network: visit hospitals and help people. Simple, easy, meaningful, and new endless networks. Think outside of the box. Soon I pray….

#readyforclass #canihelp #spencerblue #rescue #pleaseadopt

THINK OUTSIDE THE BOX

My son wanted to try out for a private lacrosse league. It involved going to four different states for tournaments. Most parents would see travel expenses, time away from home, the hours of driving. I say YES! This is like hitting the lottery for me in the world of networking when we travel: 4 new hotels, 4 new fields of parents I don't know, meeting families of the new team members- sign us up!

My boys. They are **networking magnets**. Sports, school, friends ....opportunities all around for growing my network. My oldest posted a selfie on Snapchat where he had on an acne mask. 2 new inquiries and 2 new orders. My youngest is very fair and is a walking billboard for our sunscreen and sensitive skin treatments. He's always ready to share a before and after of his red cheeks from skiing! My middle son does live videos all of the time to show his acne regimen routine. I posted a before and after of his back and chest just this month and from that one snapshot, I got four orders (yes, I split the commission with him). Now that his skin is clear, I swear he sneaks chocolate to try and break out so he can make more money. Stinker.

My husband is not a social media fan, but he does contribute as a connector when it comes to my business. Partners can be one of three Cs: **Customers, Connectors, or Consultants.** He is a customer but for sure does not run around telling everyone he steals my goods. But yes, he CONNECTS me to people. In the beginning, he would run around and say, "This shit works!" so we had to nip that sales tactic in the bud real quick. Probably not the best tag line. Now, he simply will put me in contact with friends, or friends' wives, who he thinks may be looking for products or an opportunity. How does he know this? By simply talking to his buddies or co-workers.

EVEN **online groups** with Facebook, Instagram, Follow Tik Tokkers or find commonalities on any social platform. *Disclaimer- Tik- Tokkers may be a boomer term I just created.* I am a boy mom, dog lover, wine drinker, go-getter, so I should be part of groups that are about boys, a group about dogs, and a group about wines. If there is no group for go-getters, go MAKE one. Go find groups and ways to connect on social media and start *interacting*. Do not go into those groups and spam them with your business. Great way to get the boot out. Be of value. Not have it in your mind that you want them all on your team, just connect and start a relationship. The rest will follow whether they see your home page, social media, ask you questions, stalk you back, or wait for the right time to start the conversation when they ask you, "So, what do you do?"

Get out of the house and in front of peoples' faces, or half-face and half mask right now. Get back to connecting with people in person. You will find that it's a lot easier to form an INSTANT relationship and connection in person, rather than screen to screen. Go to networking lunches, go to fundraisers, go to the mall, and don't come home until you have met two new people. I like to play the sample game: "OK, Heather, you cannot go home until you have 2 samples in 2 peoples' hands." It's fun. It's a challenge and can work for you. Go to parties. Go to weddings. Go to baby showers, even if it's the 5th shower of the week. Go to girls' or guys' nights out. Go to funerals (*Disclaimer-ok maybe not there for networking…was just following the stages of life in that line*).

Remember, samples work. So while you are out networking, always have samples on hand. The sample in the mail got me. The sample at the pool got my dear friend who is also very successful. People will try and people will buy. If you are not ordering samples every month, you are not getting enough out there into peoples' hands (if your company has samples, of course). Keep in mind with those samples, never give one away without getting contact information for that person. I remember handing samples out with cards attached to them and sit and wait for the phone to ring for their order- blahahahhahaha. NOPE! Not how it works. Life happens and life is busy so try on the 8-12 touch! It's sales! It's that way for everyone and every industry. How about you connect right then and there on a social media platform? You can be in touch 8 to 12 times before expecting a sale.

If you are connected on social media platforms, they will now see your awesome "Showing" posts not "telling" posts and they will inquire, right? If you do not continuously follow up, you are setting the sale or close up FOR SOMEONE ELSE. Sucks when that happens and it will, so find your way to organizing those follow-ups. I am an old school- still paper and notebook kind of person. You need to be recording and writing down the names of your new friends so you can follow up! Even if you don't generally like people☺ go make friends. Do not cross off their name, from your list, until they are a customer, on your team, or dead.

CHAPTER 16 - PREPARING FOR FLIGHT...

It's 11:38 PM Thursday. I have gotten up to go to the bathroom when I didn't have to go. I have pet #Spencerblue so many times he thinks I am leaving for vacation or something. My lips look like a cross between a planet with craters and a brain, riddled with cold sores. The stress of the world today, the job loss, the kids' home all the time, the worrying has taken a hit on my body. But I know me. I am afraid. I am procrastinating. What if I fail? What if this book blows?

What if...

I am afraid because I am paragraphs away from finishing this book. But I am TERRIFIED because I told Margaret, you know- my therapist, this morning that "I wrote a book". I would be lying if I don't finish because it's almost midnight. "Wrote" is past tense. I need to finish.

Up until this morning when I told her, not one person has known I am writing this. Not one. Why did I tell Margaret? Not because she said she would read it, but because telling her would hold me accountable. See, still using my strategies. I could click 'save' and leave these words in my MAC. Now she knows, and she will follow up and this will force me to the next step. Putting it out there.

Just do it. What is the worst that can happen? It never gets printed......so what! The three weeks of writing have kept me sane during this craziness. That is reason enough. The 9 years of training in the shower transferred to a book where maybe my teaching will live on. It's made me slow down. It's made me reflect on my journey, that now, I can appreciate even more.

If it weren't for this business, I may still be teaching. This means I would be online teaching, hybrid teaching, teaching from home, leaving my kids to fend for themselves, being stressed more at night, all the while helping other students while my children sank into the depths of COVID 2020 blackness.

Instead, I am making them breakfast. I am here for questions about their work. I am here for lunch and maybe sneak some ice-cream, and help when the wifi world wants to be moody. Car rides to practices and maybe some chatting. I am here.

I am here teaching. When they work on their class Zooms, I type here...teaching YOU. And anyone who may have picked up this book to learn and to see, you can do this. Whatever your "this" is.

If you need a change, **make a move**. The worst place you can be is "the same" place if it's not EXACTLY where you want to be.

I KNOW I have it all: I am teaching on my terms, I am home, and if you are reading this, I may be inspiring someone.

What if **you** fly?

CHAPTER 17 - CUSTOMER SERVICE AND SALES TIPS

LOL saved the most boring to write about for last but a MUST HAVE for running an awesome business. Customer service is a sure bonus. *Disclaimer- in my rough draft this page is page 69 so I would have to write another page anyhow. Can't leave on page 69! That's a teacher 'no-no'.*

Giving your customers service, and EXTRA service, is what makes you stand out from any other purchase they probably made yesterday, today, and will tomorrow. Online ordering is the way of now and will be forever. *YOU are the different. So, make the difference.* You make this transaction special. I have enjoyed the customer service aspect of this job, very surprisingly. I am not sure why really. I dealt with customers when I worked at the Hallmark Cards store, but I was always happy because I was constantly eating the chocolates by the register for 3 years. I mean come on- chocolate? So, here are some ideas that worked for me…

CARDS: (speaking of cards)

When you get a new client, send them a thank you or welcome card. It is so special to get something in the mail other than a BILL, let alone something handwritten where you had to go buy a stamp and then put it in the mailbox??? HOLY EFFORT! But that is exactly what your new client knows you had to do. All of that and it is effort these days. Too easy to just send a text, so send a card. Lord, go to the Dollar Stores- theirs are nice! Over the holidays, send your best clients a little gift; a coffee gift card, a donation in their name, or even just a card...a family picture... just to let them know they are on your holiday list. Such a sweet, simple gesture that has nothing to do with making a sale. But they will lead to more buying.

Fries with that?

Ever wonder why McDonald's constantly asks if you want fries with your order? Cause most people say yes. That marketing is one of the most successful... "Would you like fries with that?" You should be using this sales tactic with your sales. No- not really for fries, but for any product your client may not know you have. I would bet probably half of my clients don't even go to my site because I help them with orders, so they need to be asked. "Would you like gauze pads, too? How about a cleansing mask? Winter is approaching how about you fill your lip serums?" And so on....When you upsell and teach your team to upsell, you get more products into their hands, they will love them, and more volume in your organization. Simple! You're welcome.

Make them feel special

Who? Your clients and your team. Or anyone who has supported you and your journey. Your clients need to know their orders are appreciated and your team needs to hear that their efforts are seen and also appreciated. If your clients feel appreciated, they will help you. Have them post for you on social media. "Hey, friends! I bought this new flat iron from my friend, Shanaynay. It's the best I have ever tried ....and so no". Instant third-party validation right there. Have them host events- online are so easy and a way to reach thousands from your couch with a click. Your team can be told thank you, also send cards, congratulate them on social media, run fun contests with rewards...even contests for action items not necessarily just closing sales. Reward the activity. Local team? Host a luncheon where you serve the "Power Salad" (so awesome- see my website).

VIP page

The VIP page can be a really cool place. Make some kind of page for your clients. Or even a website- you can find free, easy website builders in minutes, hence mine below. Here, you post specials and tutorials on what you are selling. But you *also want to post other information* that has nothing to do with your product, but everything to do with helping your clients. Favorite new on- the- go recipe? Share it. New beauty trick like 'the tinkle'? Share it. (not the hairspray move I made- the tinkle- see my site. You will thank me.) New favorite winter hat? Share it. Ask your clients to invite their friends that you can now call future clients☺.

Be a billboard

If you are not using, or wearing, or showcasing, or whatever you are selling, you are doing a huge injustice to your company and your clients. Weight loss products? I want to see the before and after. Pants that make your butt look amazing? I want to see pics and send me a pair. Oils? I want to read testimonials. You get the idea. My picture below pretty much sums out how I feel about being a billboard☺.

Chapter 18- THE NOT SO SECRET RECIPE

I am probably asked weekly, "What is your secret?" I don't have one. Neither does anyone in networking marketing because there is no secret. *My secret* is, right now, the 26,013 words so far I have shared with you in this book. If I am going to say there is any kind of recipe, however, it is the below. Follow the system, or recipe outlined by me below. I was a carbon cut out of this system. Thanks, Jenn, my momma love.

- Meet people (in person or social media)
- make a connection
- listen to TINY or look for one based on their profile/posting
- offer the products/business when appropriate/without spraying perfume
- get them a sample or using a product
- follow up
- invite them to an event where they can learn more (third party validation be present)

Do not cross them off your list until they are a customer, on your team…or dead

Enjoy your journey and give your opportunity to all.

I weighed myself this morning. Weigh-ins are on Monday mornings, how convenient. I guess it keeps you in line over the weekend. I am down 18 pounds, the healthy way that does not include extreme measures…old school weight watchers! I have also been walking a lot, but there has been one change to my walking routine that helped initiate this book. Instead of popping in my earbuds and blasting the music I used to listen to while training for the marathon, I started listening to youtube videos on everything; anything inspirational, motivational, anything uplifting.

I was not in the best place about 6 weeks ago. Struggling with working from home, kids' school changing, and frustrated with them missing out, so much was out of my control, husband's recent job loss in this horrid COVID crap, the list goes on. I needed something to do. Something new to focus on. I was probably on my third loop around this empty field with #spencerblue when I looked up and saw a rainbow. It wasn't even raining. It didn't rain before or after! The rainbow was clearly there, and it seemed to be landing on my car. My car was a gift, a trophy from the company I had dedicated the past 9 years to. I have always had the itch to write. I have always had a passion for teaching. It was that one lap around the field where I was saying to myself, "What can I do now?"

You just finished reading the universe's answer. This book, start to finish in 30 days, was the outcome of that walk, that rainbow, a feeling of being lost, and the desire to keep teaching, all while keeping me sane during the most difficult of times. **There's always a ray of light somewhere, you just need to look.**

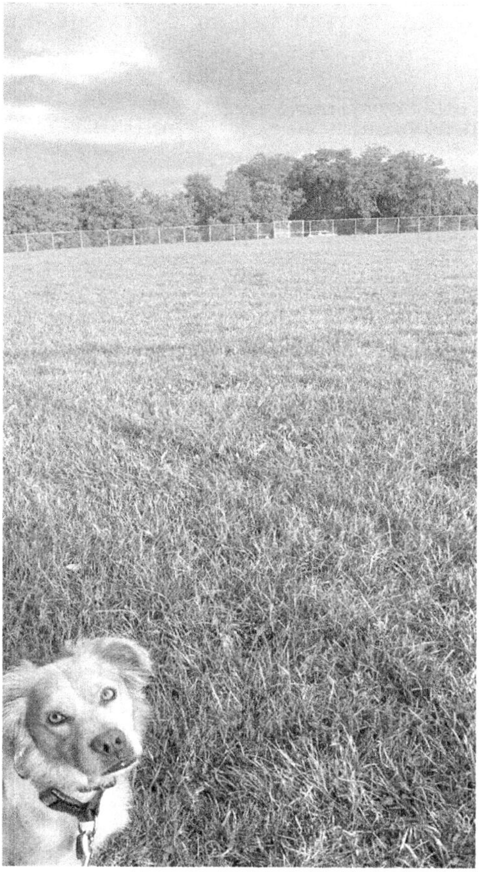

Made in the USA
Monee, IL
15 October 2020